CCDA THEOLOGICAL
JOURNAL 2014 EDITION

EDITED BY

Soong-Chan Rah
Chanequa Walker-Barnes
Brandon Wrencher

CCDA
PUBLISHING
WWW.CCDA.ORG

CCDA Theology Committee

The purpose of the CCDA Theology Committee is to articulate the theological foundations of Christian community development and to foster theological engagement within and beyond the community of CCDA.

The committee's primary work has been to produce the CCDA Theological Journal.

Soong-Chan Rah—Co-Chair
Chanequa Walker-Barnes—Co-Chair
Vince Bantu
Mae Cannon
M. Daniel Carroll R.
Dominique Gillard
Jonathan Blackburn
Bethany Harris

Contents

Part III: Book Reviews

Letter from the Editors

Welcome to the third annual issue of the CCDA Theological Journal. The Theological Committee of the CCDA is pleased to present this volume on the 2014 CCDA national conference theme of "Flourish." The theme has the possibility of a wide range of meaning with a potential for a variety of applications. The theme also holds potential for great misapplication. This year's journal presents biblical, historical, and theological articles on the topic for your consideration as a CCDA community.

Our first section presents four different scholars examining the theme of "Flourish." Jim Bruckner is Professor of Old Testament at North Park Theological Seminary in Chicago, IL. Dr. Bruckner was raised in an indigenous community in Alaska and his article reflects his concern for the community as well as careful biblical reflection. Dr. Bruckner also authored of one of the most important books on the topic of human flourishing, *Healthy Human Life: A Biblical Witness*.

Rev. Dr. Dennis Edwards is a pastor-scholar who pastors an urban church and holds a PhD in Biblical Studies. Rev. Dr. Edwards serves as the senior pastor of Sanctuary Covenant Church in Minneapolis, Minnesota. Rev. Dr. Edwards not only brings a scholar's care in exegeting the passage, but also applies the passage with pastoral sensitivity and ministry experience insights.

Kate Bowler is Assistant Professor of the History of Christianity in the United States at Duke University. Dr. Bowler is the foremost scholar on the topic of prosperity theology in the North American context. Her recent publication, *Blessed* (Oxford, 2013) now serves as the definitive work on the history of the North American expression of prosperity theology. Dr. Bowler's article for this volume provides an academically balanced and essential historical reflection on the topic.

Valerie Landfair is a PhD student at Regent University in the field of Pentecostal studies with particular emphasis on silence and lament theology. Ms. Landfair, a former student of the late Ogbu Kalu, reflects on Dr. Kalu's work on global Pentecostalism, which offers a different angle on prosperity theology.

This year's volume offers a new, but hopefully an ongoing feature of upcoming journals. The CCDA Theology Committee reviewed ten different articles submitted by the CCDA community and picked two articles that best addressed our topic. We are thankful to Allie Wong and Samantha Domingo for their contributions to the journal.

Our journal once again incorporates articles that focus on CCDA work in our host state of North Carolina. Chas Edens, the Executive Director at Anathoth Community Farm and Garden in Cedar Grove, and Reynolds Chapman, a church planter who's been active in Durham's Walltown community and with Moral Mondays, both bear witness to God's work of reconciliation and justice through their community development ministry in North Carolina.

We also offer three book reviews on works that offer relevant ministry application for the CCDA community. CCDA is blessed to have insightful authors in our midst. Mae Cannon, Lisa Sharon Harper, Troy Jackson, and Soong-Chan Rah have co-authored *Forgive Us: Confessions of a Compromised Faith* (Zondervan, 2014). The content of this book has been introduced in previous CCDA National Conferences and is now available as a text. Margot Starbuck offers a review of *Forgive Us*. CCDA Board member Chanequa Walker Barnes has authored *Too Heavy a Yoke: Black Women and the Burden of Strength* (Cascade, 2014) and her book is reviewed by Nilwona Nowlin. Alexia Salvatierra and Peter Heltzel's work, *Faith-Rooted Organizing: Mobilizing the Church in Service to the World* (IVP Books, 2013) is reviewed by Anthony Grimes. All three book reviews should spur the journal reader to further their inquiry on these topics.

EDITORS:
Soong-Chan Rah
Chanequa Walker-Barnes
Brandon Wrencher

ON BEHALF OF THE THEOLOGY COMMITTEE OF THE CCDA:
Vince Bantu
Jonathan Blackburn
Mae Elise Cannon
M. Daniel Carroll R.
Dominique Gilliard
Bethany Harris

Part I

CCDA National Conference Theme:
"Flourishing"

PROSPERITY AND FLOURISHING

A BIBLICAL WITNESS

JAMES K. BRUCKNER

Introduction

My first encounter with prosperity-gospel preaching was on late-night Chicago radio in the mid-1970s, as a young college student. Rev. Ike almost convinced me that I could, by a word of faith and a righteous donation, reach out and touch-to-own a fine new car, regardless of my meager funds. "You can't lose with the stuff I use," he cajoled in Jesus' name. The lure of gold for those who need bread is as old as the hills themselves. What is true "prosperity"?

In the indigenous community that raised me, gold is a natural phenomenon of the local hills and streams. The gold rush that tore the lives and the land is long over, but the rich wisdom of the people remains: "Don't try to get rich from gold. It will ruin your family." A little gold to buy tools and tea is enough. But now, the major challenge to this wisdom has begun again. The proposed Pebble Mine's massive gold deposits lie deep beneath the surface in western Alaska. The problem is that the surface "over-load" is the richest salmon spawning and hatching ground in the world.[1] Measured in dollars, the gold is worth much more than many annual salmon harvests.

What will the people of the land (and the state and federal governments) decide? The salmon support a trickle economy that is the life-blood of the Native-Alaskan cultures. It is also the source of the last major wild-salmon fishery in the world. The gold would create great wealth for the state, the mining companies, and for some of the people. For what shall we pray? The choices each require faith and trust in the

---

1. "Pebble" is an ironically diminutive name for a gold mine that would affect thousands of square miles of isolated watershed spawning ground. The "over-load" is the ground that would have to be moved to access the metals. The gold and copper are estimated to have a value in excess of 150 *billion* dollars. For a fact sheet, see http://www.aktrekking.com/pebble/facts.html.

promised outcomes. But the goals of that faith and trust are quite different from one another.

Health and wealth gospel preachers also make great promises delivered through faith and trust. But faith and trust in *what?* Their promises are quite different from the promises of Scripture and the true Gospel of Jesus the Christ. In the *Torah*, prosperity and blessing are measured by how well the destitute poor, fatherless, immigrants, and widows are faring in the neighborhood. True prosperity and blessing are *never* measured by how well the religious elite are paid. The prosperity-gospel has more in common with the baalisms of the Old Testament than with either *torah*-justice or the Jesus-Gospel.[2] Baalism's success is measured by the prosperity of baalism's prophets.

The Problem: "The Worst Idea of the Decade"

True prosperity and flourishing in Scripture is always rooted in an awareness of our vulnerability as created and redeemed by God. It is a partnership with God in the embrace of the more vulnerable and it understands the threat of re-enslavement to false notions of health, wealth, and success. Cathleen Falsani's *Washington Post* article calls the prosperity-gospel "The Worst Idea of the Decade."

> Few theological ideas ring more dissonant with the harmony of orthodox Christianity than a focus on storing up treasures on earth as a primary goal of faithful living. The gospel of prosperity turns Christianity into a vapid bless-me club, with a doctrine that amounts to little more than spiritual magical thinking: If you pray the right way, God will make you rich.[3]

Scot McKnight calls its theology "a half-truth, perhaps less." We are called to a "cross-gospel" not a prosperity-gospel and its "vending machine God."[4]

False and alternate gospels are nothing new. The presenting problem of the prosperity-gospel (besides being false) is that people in our poorest communities are being deceived. This false American gospel is now being exported to poor communities in Africa and the Philippines by preachers who stay only long enough to profit. The *warnings* against a focus on material wealth as the object of faith are strong and replete in Scripture. For example,

> Those who want to get rich fall into temptation and a snare and many foolish and harmful desires which plunge men into ruin and destruction. For the love

2. M. Daniel Carroll Rodas, "Cultivating Oaks of Righteousness: Restoration and Mission in Isaiah 61" *CCDA Theological Journal* 2 (2013): 5–10.

3. Cathleen Falsani is the religion columnist for the Chicago Sun-Times. Cathleen Falsani, "The Worst Ideas of the Decade: the prosperity gospel," *Washington Post*, Internet, available from http://www.washingtonpost.com/wp-srv/special/opinions/outlook/worst-ideas/prosperity-gospel.html.

4. Scot McKnight, "The Problem for the Prosperity Gospel," *Beliefnet*, Internet, available from http://www.beliefnet.com/Faiths/Christianity/2009/03/The-Problem-for-the-Prosperity-Gospel.aspx.

of money is a root of all sorts of evil, and some by longing for it have wandered away from the faith, and pierced themselves with many a pang. But flee from these things, you man of God; and pursue righteousness, godliness, faith, love, perseverance and gentleness. (1 Tim. 6:9–11; NAS throughout)

Then there are Jesus' words: "You cannot serve God and money" (Matt. 6:24; Lk. 16:3). Jesus' words for the rich are clear: "It is easier for a camel to go through the eye of a needle, than for a rich man to enter the kingdom of God" (Matt. 19:24). Those with earthly wealth are warned to put their hope in true riches and true life.

Command those who are rich in this present world not to be arrogant nor to put their hope in wealth, which is so uncertain, but to put their hope in God . . . Command them to do good, to be *rich in good deeds*, and to be generous and willing to share. *In this way they will lay up treasure* for themselves as a firm foundation for the coming age, so that they may take hold of the *life that is truly life*." (1 Tim. 6:17–19)

The biblical call is for the well-to-do to be downwardly, not upwardly, mobile in relation to neighborhoods of suffering. It gives us dignity, hope, and real help in the midst of suffering communities (Phil. 2:1–13). The measure of a truly rich community is the condition of the local poor. The effects of the LORD's *torah*-righteousness on the poor, administered by a good Davidic king in an ancient community, are described in Psalm 72.

For he will deliver the needy when he cries for help, the afflicted also, and him who has no helper. He will have compassion on the poor and needy, and the lives of the needy he will save. He will rescue their life from oppression and violence; and their blood will be precious in his sight . . . May those from the city flourish like vegetation of the earth. (Ps. 72:12–14, 16)

A prospering community gained through participation in the LORD's *torah*-righteousness and justice and focused by a hope in the Kingdom of God (Matt. 5–7) *is not the same as* an individualized prosperity gained through a word of faith and by giving money to church leaders.[5]

Blessed in Order To Be a Blessing: the Older Testament Witness

And yet, were not Abraham and Solomon *rich*? Doesn't God the King want to bless his children? Blessing in the OT is often misused as a warrant for prosperity thinking. The purpose of biblical blessing and election, however, is not health and wealth, or even the blessing itself. God's calling, blessing, and election of Abram, Sarai, Jacob,

5. The false hope of earthly treasure as the inheritance due to "children of the King" is a misappropriated realized eschatology. Cf. Soong-Chan Rah's discussion of "misappropriated Christology" in Soong-Chan Rah, "Rethinking Incarnational Ministry" *CCDA Theological Journal* 2 (2013): 31–37.

Rachel, Leah, Joseph, and Moses was that they might become participants in God's intention to set communities free from human abuses and strife, reconciling the world to himself one tribe at a time.

God blessed Abraham with repeated promises (Gen. 12, 15, 17, 18, 22) so that he "might be a blessing to the ethnicities" (Gr: *ethnos*; Heb: *goyim*) of the world. He used his wealth and power to rescue Lot and captives from five towns (including Sodom and Gomorrah) from southern traffickers (Gen. 14). Jacob's blessing was a struggle that resulted in his reconciliation with Esau and Edom, and came with a limp as an enduring symbol. Joseph's blessing began in bondage and his participation in a struggle for integrity. Its purpose and his participation led to the salvation, not simply of his tribe, but of the whole nation of Egypt. Moses' blessing also led through privation, struggle, and the deliverance of a nation from chattel slavery. True visualization and words of faith for blessing are never focused on achieving financial success. They are visions that engage us in bond-breaking, reconciling, and deliverance ministries in plagued neighborhoods of the world.

Prosperity and Baalism

In ancient Israel, Ba'al and Yahweh (a.k.a., "The LORD") had many similarities to the casual observer. Each provided rain for the crops, causing grapes, figs, and olives to grow. Each gave flocks pasture and increase. Each protected their worshipers, providing health and wealth. All that was required of people with these faiths was to bring an offering to the priests to be sure you were on each god's success ledger. It is no wonder that the harmony of Yahweh and the Ba'al was preached at the baalistic northern sanctuaries.[6] But *baalism's* prosperity is measured, by definition, by financial success. Biblical Yahwehism, however, measured and visualized prosperity quite differently. The primary difference between them was the Sinaitic *torah*.

Sinai's instruction (*torah*) *actually provided for* the health, protection, and the true prospering of the weakest members of the community. When the *torah*-justice of Sinai was not taught, they were easily fooled into a magic-like prosperity thinking: speak a word of faith; bring an offering to the pastor/priest; receive God's financial blessing. The thin theology of a contract with a false god leads to thin hope. For Israel, it led to catastrophe and exile.

Prosperity-gospel religion has many natural forms throughout the cultures of the world. Whether you barter with a shaman or pay a priest, the intent is similar: to gain improvement of your circumstance. This is the basic common shape of religion. We ought not fault the poor for pursuing the means they know to improve their life and security. But there is a far more substantive foundation for flourishing than individual negotiations with God for money.

6. See Patrick Miller, "Yahwehism and Cult" in *The Religion of Ancient Israel* (Louisville: Westminster John Knox Press, 2000), 46–86.

This *torah* foundation, fully interpreted in Jesus' teaching, is God's own initiative to save and recruit a people to participate in saving acts of justice. This *pathos* of God is the root of the gospel in both testaments. God's intention to bless the world is revealed in the *torah* narrative and Sinai instruction, the preaching prophet's reiteration of the *torah*, and the wisdom of the OT writings, fully manifest in Jesus' teaching, death, and resurrection. True worship and true prosperity from the LORD (Yahweh) are experienced in communities that participate in this *pathos*. Exodus 22 represents God's primary passion for justice. The LORD says,

> You shall not wrong a stranger or oppress him, for you were strangers in the land of Egypt. You shall not afflict any widow or orphan. If you afflict him at all, and if he does cry out to me, I will surely hear his cry; and my anger will be kindled, and I will kill you with the sword; . . . If you lend money to my people, to the poor among you, you are not to act as a creditor to him; you shall not charge him interest. (Exod. 22:21–25)

Today, prosperity-gospel preachers use the blessings of Deuteronomy 28 (e.g., v. 11: "The LORD will make you abound in prosperity") as motivating fodder for visualizing a better life. This use of Deuteronomy is half-right: it is a motivation, but in context, it is not the primary goal. The primary purpose of the blessing is so God's people might keep the Lord's vision for a prospering neighborhood (Deut 28:1). Specifically listed are laws of protection for elders, the blind, vulnerable women, aliens, orphans, widows, animals, and weak neighbors (Deut. 27:15–26).

Deuteronomic prosperity, health, and wealth are not given as ends in themselves, nor "by a word of faith," positive confession, and visualization, but as a potential by-product of participating in God's restorative work in the neighborhoods of the world (a.k.a. "righteousness"). Wealth itself is marked as a primary danger and a threat to true prosperity and success in the LORD's community of faith. Moses gives dire warnings about the dangers of wealth becoming a self-authenticating goal (Deut. 8:11–14, 17–18; 30:1–10). Jeremiah condemns the prophets of the LORD who preach a false prosperity and success to the people remaining in Jerusalem (Jer. 29:8–9, 21–23). This false teaching unnecessarily led to the Babylonian siege and increased suffering of the common people. True prosperity was to be found in building a new community of faith in Babylon (Jer. 29:4–7).

When American baalisms of health and wealth become the focus of our "words of faith," the "faith" that is visualized is not Christian, but is a false hope in a magical cure. Solomon, the wealthiest, most *blessed* man in Scripture, is held up as a moral tale by the deuteronomist, for his failure to keep God's torah vision for a healthy community. At the moment of his greatest success and glory, the dedication of the first Temple, he prays five words of warning that echo down the monarchial history.[7] The

---

7. 1 Kings 8:30, 31–34, 35–36, 37–40, 47–50. Generally, "When they sin, the community falls apart, and they cry out to you, please forgive them and restore them."

deuteronomic editor made sure there would be no confusion about the focus and purpose of Israel's successes, health, and wealth: the faithful work for a community based on *torah*-justice (1 Kings 8:56–61). Solomon's sad end is his own failure to make the distinction between his own successes, wealth, and wisdom and the LORD's *torah*-justice intention for the people he ruled.

True Health, Flourishing, and Strength

So what does a blessed and a thriving life look like? What does it mean to thrive, flourish, and be strong in the midst of suffering or struggling communities? "Strength" is a peculiar word in the famous *Shema* text (Deut. 6:5). It is the adverb "very" (Heb: *me'od*). "You shall love the LORD your God . . . with all your *very*! Many other Hebrew words for "strength" could have been used, but this one leaves the translation possibilities open, including "thriving," "flourishing," and "vitality."[8] "You shall love the LORD your God with all your *thriving*."

The primary context of the meaning of "strength" (*me'od*) in Scripture is counterintuitive to our ordinary ways of thinking. It is gained in telling the truth of our mutual vulnerability, our dependence on God, and on each other.[9]

I Need You To Survive

Human beings are fundamentally vulnerable and dependent on each other for their survival. A truly healthy community acknowledges this dependence and vulnerability. Our American culture often teaches the opposite values: that I may flourish if I am independent and secured from any vulnerability.[10] Struggling communities know and can teach that we are not yet fully aware of our radical dependence on others or aware of ourselves as vulnerable.[11]

We are always somewhere on a continuum between dependence and ability, in need of a helping community for our vitality and growth. "Throughout our lives, from infancy to old age, we move back and forth along this scale."[12] Healthy communities

8. The call of the *Shema* is to "Love the LORD your God with all your heart, with all your soul, *and with all your strength* (*me'od*)." What follows in this article is a version of part of chapter six, "What is Strength?" in James K. Bruckner, *Healthy Human Life: A Biblical Witness* (Eugene, OR: Wipf & Stock, 2012).

9. Ibid. See chapter eight, "Telling the Truth in Suffering" on biblical resources for community lament.

10. Alasdair C. MacIntyre, *Dependent Rational Animals: Why Human Beings Need the Virtues* (Chicago: Open Court, 1999), 135.

11. Ibid, 136–38. MacIntyre finds the most compelling evidence in irrational responses of revulsion that people have to a person with facial disfigurement. They are made in the image of God but we are repulsed, even knowing better. He argues that we can gain both self-awareness and a new vitality from what they have to teach us by their presence and experience.

12. See discussion in Warren Brown, "Human Nature, Physicalism, Spirituality, and Healing:

acknowledge this dependence and provide for those who are in seasons or conditions of more extreme dependence. Flourishing depends on the self-awareness, imagination, and visioning of a community.[13]

The Strength of Brokenness

Every community and every person that acknowledges brokenness has the possibility of *meʾod*—strength: vitality, flourishing, and thriving through the body of Christ. Christian identity and knowledge is established primarily by Christ's body, broken for our sake. This shift in identity away from normal cultural standards of thriving to the blessed-broken body of Christ is in itself an experience of wonder and transformation. For this reason the Lord's Supper is a strong and sustaining practice in Christian worship.

Brokenness lies at the heart of this new counter-intuitive definition of thriving and strength.[14] Vitality of life comes through death: Jesus' death and the death and re-birth of human identity in Christ.[15] The strength of the *very* is made possible through human weakness.

The apostle Paul suffered an unknown disability, even as the early church struggled against all odds. He used this as an occasion to teach the central perspective of a *better strength* that is possible for those who are aware of their disability as a source of strength. This revelation came to him in God's words within an experience of wonder: "My grace is sufficient for you, for power is made perfect in weakness." His insight for the Corinthian community was an embodiment of the gospel (2 Cor. 12:9–10; see Rom. 8:26; 2 Cor. 11:30).

Power can be perfected in weakness because a relationship with God is possible, no matter who we are, because we can offer our praise and thanks. We may embrace this fundamental vocation in our created potential to share in the transcendent life of God within God's community of love and respect. The psalmist calls us to this thriving vocation:

> I will bless the LORD at all times; his praise shall continually be in my mouth.
> My life makes its boast in the LORD; let the afflicted hear and be glad. O
> magnify the LORD with me, and let us exalt his Name together. (Ps. 34:1–3)

This invitation to the afflicted, to join in praise through the ages, reflects the joyful experience of wonder and glory in the midst of his weakness and suffering.[16] It describes

---

Theological View of a Neuroscientist" *Ex Auditu* 21 (2005): 121–22.

13. The exclusion of the severely disabled as "a fact of nature" obscures the actual fact that "the obstacles presented by those afflictions can be overcome . . . What disability amounts to . . . depends not just on the disabled individual, but on the groups of which that individual is a member." MacIntyre, *Dependent Rational Animals*, 75.

14. *Christian Perspectives on Theological Anthropology: A Faith and Order Study Document*, Faith and Order Papers, 199 (Geneva: World Council of Churches, 2005), 26.

15. Rom. 6:3–5; Col. 2:12; In 1 Cor. 15:30 Paul can say, "I die every day."

16. See also, for example, Lamentations 3:18–24.

the ultimate vocation of all created in God's image, to be in communication with the Creator; to be empowered and transformed, no matter the circumstance.

A community can be transformed out of a health and wealth false-gospel ideology of independence, autonomy, and false securities when it embraces an ethos of love for the vulnerable, builds a neighborhood of respect for all, and has, at its center, the praise of the LORD.

BIBLIOGRAPHY

Brown, Warren. "Human Nature, Physicalism, Spirituality, and Healing: Theological View of a Neuroscientist." *Ex Auditu* 21 (2005): 112–27.

Bruckner, James K. *Healthy Human Life: A Biblical Witness*. Eugene, OR: Wipf & Stock, 2012.

Carroll Rodas, M. Daniel. "Cultivating Oaks of Righteousness: Restoration and Mission in Isaiah 61." *CCDA Theological Journal* 2 (2013): 5–10.

Christian Perspectives on Theological Anthropology: A Faith and Order Study Document. Faith and Order Papers. 199. Geneva: World Council of Churches, 2005.

MacIntyre, Alasdair C. *Dependent Rational Animals: Why Human Beings Need the Virtues*. Chicago: Open Court, 1999.

Miller, Patrick. *The Religion of Ancient Israel*. Louisville: Westminster John Knox Press, 2000.

Rah, Soong-Chan. "Rethinking Incarnational Ministry." *CCDA Theological Journal* 2 (2013): 31–37.

FLOURISHING

DENNIS EDWARDS

Urban life is complex and often difficult. Yet, more than half the world's population lives in urban areas, including some 69% of Americans.[1] As an urban pastor and theologian, I have often wondered what it means for God's people to experience an abundant life. Jesus says, "The thief comes only to steal and kill and destroy. I came that they may have life, and have it abundantly" (John 10:10). An abundant life is a life that flourishes. To flourish, according to a dictionary definition, is to "grow or develop in a healthy or vigorous way, especially as the result of a particularly favorable environment."[2] I have come to believe that God intends for his people to grow in healthy and vigorous ways even though the environment may not always be favorable. The key to such flourishing is found in the understanding and practice of God's *shalom*.[3] God's peace, or *shalom*, is found through developing a meaningful relationship with God that is practiced within the life of Christian community.

It is the ongoing work of Christian faith to consider the various ways that we develop a meaningful relationship with God, so it is impossible to exhaust such matters in a few pages. However, this paper will examine aspects of the notion of flourishing by considering the context in which peace may be found: genuine community.

Jeremiah 29 provides a backdrop, but this paper emphasizes NT teaching. I will briefly consider our context as resident aliens, our call to flourish as part of a

---

1. "Urban Population," *The Henry J. Kaiser Family Foundation*, Internet, available from http://kff.org/global-indicator/urban-population/, accessed May 8, 2014.

2. *Oxford Dictionaries*, Internet, available from http://www.oxforddictionaries.com/us/definition/american_english/flourish, accessed May 8, 2014.

3. There are lots of places to which one may turn for discussions of *shalom*. For thorough biblical analyses, see Willard M. Swartley, *Covenant of Peace: The Missing Peace in New Testament Theology and Ethics* (Grand Rapids: Eerdmans, 2006); Shemaryahu Talmon, "The Significance of Shalom and its Semantic Field in the Hebrew Bible," in *The Quest for Context and Meaning: Studies in Biblical Intertextuality in Honor of James A. Sanders*, ed. Craig Evans and Talmon Shemaryahu (Leiden: Brill, 1997), 75–115.

community, and our role in contributing to the overall flourishing of our world, even though we are ultimately citizens of heaven (e.g. Phil 3:20).

God's People are Resident Aliens

About 586 years before Jesus was born in Bethlehem, the prophet Jeremiah wrote a letter to beleaguered Judeans who had been dragged from their homes by King Nebuchadnezzar's army. In that letter, found in Jeremiah 29, the weeping prophet famously offers the exiles words that they surely did not want to hear:

> Thus says the LORD of hosts, the God of Israel, to all the exiles whom I have sent into exile from Jerusalem to Babylon: Build houses and live in them; plant gardens and eat what they produce. Take wives and have sons and daughters; take wives for your sons, and give your daughters in marriage, that they may bear sons and daughters; multiply there, and do not decrease. But seek the welfare of the city where I have sent you into exile, and pray to the LORD on its behalf, for in its welfare you will find your welfare. (Jer 29:4–8)[4]

Instead of instigating a revolt or promising a short time of trouble (as the false prophets had done), Jeremiah said what amounts to a slogan: "As Babylon's life goes, so goes your life!" The exiles were to carry on with their lives—even while being far from the land of promise. They were not living in a favorable environment, yet God still intended for them to flourish, as Jer 29:11 shows: "For surely I know the plans I have for you, says the LORD, plans for your welfare and not for harm, to give you a future with hope."

Even though Christians—particularly in the Western Hemisphere—have not been dragged off to a strange land, we may also be considered to be exiles, or resident aliens in a similar way as the OT people of God in Jeremiah's day. For example, the NT letter of 1 Peter is addressed to "the exiles of the Dispersion" (1 Pet 1:1) and ends with greetings from "Babylon" (1 Pet 5:13), an epithet for Rome. These designations suggest that both the sender and the recipients of 1 Peter are Christian believers not fully at home in the world in which they reside. As John H. Elliott suggests, "1 Peter is a letter addressed to resident aliens and visiting strangers who, since their conversion to Christianity, still find themselves estranged from any place of belonging."[5]

The apostle Paul uses different language to discuss the place of the Christians in Philippi yet gets at some of the same ideas as 1 Peter. Paul tells the Philippians "your citizenship is in heaven" (Phil 3:20). Stanley Hauerwas and William H. Willimon, in reflecting on the language of Phil 3:20, suggest that American Christians are exiles, or "resident aliens": "We believe that the designations of the church as a colony and

---

4. Scripture references are from the New Revised Standard Version.

5. John Hall Elliott, *A Home for the Homeless: A Sociological Exegesis of 1 Peter, Its Situation and Strategy* (Philadelphia: Fortress Press, 1981), 49.

Christians as resident aliens are not too strong for the modern American church—indeed, we believe it is the nature of the church, at any time and in any situation to be a colony."[6]

If space allowed we could examine more Scripture, but it is fair to say that God's people—the Church—consists of resident aliens whose true citizenship is in heaven, yet who are called to flourish in the "Babylon" of contemporary life.

It is helpful to consider how that flourishing is to take place.

God's People Flourish in Community

Hauerwas and Willimon point out:

> To be resident but alien as a formula for loneliness that few of us can sustain. Indeed, it is almost impossible to minister alone because our loneliness can too quickly turn into self-righteousness or self-hate. Christians can survive only by supporting one another through the countless small acts through which we tell one another we are not alone, that God is with us.[7]

Indeed, Hauerwas and Willimon are touching on the power of Christian community that must be experienced in order for God's resident aliens to flourish. Elsewhere I have written on the necessity of Christian community, particularly in an urban context, and will share some of those concepts here.[8]

In Phil 1:27, Apostle Paul writes "Only, live your life in a manner worthy of the gospel of Christ, so that, whether I come and see you or am absent and hear about you, I will know that you are standing firm in one spirit, striving side by side with one mind for the faith of the gospel." The main verb in that verse is *politeuomai*, which literally means, "to conduct oneself as a good citizen." Paul deliberately plays off of the concept of citizenship in the Greco-Roman world. And he does so with a group of people who were known for their devotion to Rome and their understanding of good citizenship.[9] The Philippians were urbanites who appreciated their elite status as a Roman colony. Paul takes an image that his audience understands and even celebrates, but applies it to their life together as Christian brothers and sisters.

Citizenship involved commitment to the community, to the *polis*. Aristotle wrote:

---

6. Stanley Hauerwas and William H. Willimon, *Resident Aliens: Life in the Christian Colony* (Nashville: Abingdon Press, 1989), 12.

7. Hauerwas and Willimon, *Resident Aliens*, 13.

8. See Dennis R. Edwards, "Good Citizenship: A Study of Philippians 1:27 and its Implications for Contemporary Urban Ministry," in *Ex Auditu: An International Journal of the Theological Interpretation of Scripture* 29 (2013).

9. Brewer, "The Meaning of *Politeuesthe*," observes that Paul's use of *politeuomai* and the related word *politeuma* in 3:20 "conforms to the recognized tendency of Paul to adapt his language and his thought to the varied situations he confronted in his preaching and in the pastoral care of the churches in order that he 'might by all means save some'" (83).

> Every state is as we see a sort of partnership, and every partnership is formed with a view to some good since all the actions of all mankind are done with a view to what they think to be good. It is therefore evident that, while all partnerships aim at some good the partnership that is the most supreme of all and includes all the others does so most of all, and aims at the most supreme of all goods; and this is the partnership entitled the state, the political association.[10]

Gerald F. Hawthorne interacts with Aristotle's observations and offers the following summary:

> To the ancient Greek the state (*polis*) was by no means merely a place to live. It was rather a sort of partnership (*koinœnia*) formed with a view to having people attain the highest of all human goods (so Aristotle). Here in the state the individual citizen developed his gifts and realized his potential not in isolation, but in cooperation. Here he was able to maximize his abilities not by himself, or for himself, but in community and for the good of the community . . . As a consequence, mutuality and interdependence were important ideas inhering in the concept of polis. 'To live as a citizen' (*politeuesthai*), therefore, meant for the Greek (and later the Roman) rights and privileges but also duties and responsibilities.[11]

In borrowing Paul's image of good citizenship, we can derive a model for flourishing. God's people will flourish when they see themselves functioning as "good citizens" of their heavenly home while living as resident aliens on earth. Good citizens, with respect to the Gospel of Christ, comprise healthy Christian community. Just as Jeremiah commanded that the communal life of the exiles should continue with vigor (i.e., build homes, plant gardens, have the children marry, etc), contemporary Christians must practice what makes for good community in order to flourish as God's people, wherever they may be living.

In *Community: The Structure of Belonging*, Peter Block suggests that "to improve the common measures of community health—economy, education, health, safety, the environment—we need to create a community where each citizen has the experience of being connected to those around them and knows that their safety and success are dependent on the success of all others."[12] What Block describes are aspects of what flourishing entails: the overall health of the geographic community—which includes the neighborhood in which God's people find themselves, not just the "community" of

---

10. Aristotle, *Politics, Perseus Digital Library*, Internet, available from http://www.perseus.tufts.edu/hopper/text?doc=Perseus:text:1999.01.0058, accessed May 8, 2014. The word translated "partnership" is the Greek *koinœnia*.

11. Gerald F. Hawthorne, *Philippians*, Word Biblical Commentary 43 (Waco: Word, 1983), 55. I transliterated Hawthorne's Greek.

12. Peter Block, *Community: The Structure of Belonging* (Cleveland: Berrett-Koehler Publishers, 2009), 5.

the faithful. This is like Jeremiahs' description of Babylon flourishing, which impacts God's people who live in Babylon.

In order for God's people to flourish, our aim should be to create communities of good citizens. In doing so, we will be honoring God by living out the "one another" admonitions of Scripture. But we will also be working to alleviate some of the stereotypical problems associated with contemporary life. We will also be working to activate the gifts and abilities of people—all people, regardless of social status, race, or ethnicity. And when the gifts and abilities of a variety of people are activated, it will lead to increased energy in making life better wherever God's people might be.

Flourishing takes place in community. It is in community that we learn how to relate to God as well as to each other. Part of flourishing is experiencing the peace that God intends for people—peace with him as well as peace with others.

God's People, as Peacemakers, Help Others to Flourish

Origen of Alexandria, the 3rd-Century theologian, in defending the Christian faith, wrote about how Christians contributed to the flourishing of society even when they did not participate in the Roman military. He wrote:

> Moreover, we who by our prayers destroy all daemons which stir up wars, violate oaths, and disturb the peace, are of more help to the emperors than those who seem to be doing the fighting. We who offer prayers with righteousness, together with ascetic practices and exercises which teach us to despise pleasures and not to be led by them, are cooperating in the tasks of the community. Even more do we fight on behalf of the emperor. And though we do not become fellow-soldiers with him, even if he presses for this, yet we are fighting for him and composing a special army of piety through our intercessions to God.[13]

Origen seems to be saying that Christians help the empire through spiritual practices, including prayer and upright, ethical behaviors. In a sense, that is what Jeremiah commands of the exiles in Babylon. He commands that they pray for Babylon to flourish even though they are technically not Babylonians. Contemporary believers experience God's grace and flourish in the context of Christian community, and they also contribute to the overall flourishing of society as God's peacemakers.

Peacemaking is a fundamental aspect of Christian discipleship.[14] And as peacemakers, God's people demonstrate God's love in several ways: love back toward God,

---

13. Origen, *Against Celsus*, 8.74.

14. "God gives peace that there may be peacegivers. Anyone who remains personally content with the peace of God in itself, and does not become a peacegiver, has not experienced the inward thrust of divine peace and does not know the divine Spirit." See Johann-Baptist Metz and Jurgen Moltmann, "Peace, the Fruit of Justice," in *Faith and the Future: Essays on Theology, Solidarity, and Modernity* (Maryknoll, NY: Orbis, 1995): 148.

to one another, to the stranger, and even to enemies. Communities flourish when they experience the love of God through the people of God.

As a young church planter in Brooklyn, NY, I encountered many people who appeared not to be flourishing in any sense of that word. I think of "Sam" (not his real name). He came to us in his 50s, a man with little formal education and a legacy of substance abuse and all sorts of family dysfunctions that included problems with his stepchildren and grandchildren. The small church in Brooklyn comprised of a variety of society's "misfits," learned to love each other, including Sam and his family. By the time I left that ministry, Sam testified of how much his life in Christ meant to him. He spoke about the love that he experienced in the church, demonstrated in the support and care his family received. Sam's circumstances remained difficult in many ways, but he flourished because of the peace he had with God and the peace he experienced with others.

Flourishing as exiles means finding *shalom* wherever we are, and that happens through community with God's people. And by God's grace, we exiles contribute to the overall flourishing of society, being God's peacemakers here on earth.

BIBLIOGRAPHY

Aristotle. *Politics. Perseus Digital Library*. Internet. Available from http://www.perseus.tufts.edu/hopper/text?doc=Perseus:text:1999.01.0058, accessed May 8, 2014.

Block, Peter. *Community: The Structure of Belonging*. Cleveland: Berrett-Koehler Publishers, 2009.

Elliott, John Hall. *A Home for the Homeless: A Sociological Exegesis of 1 Peter, Its Situation and Strategy*. Philadelphia: Fortress Press, 1981.

Hauerwas, Stanley and William H. Willimon. *Resident Aliens: Life in the Christian Colony*. Nashville: Abingdon Press, 1989.

Hawthorne, Gerald F. *Philippians*. Word Biblical Commentary 43. Waco: Word, 1983.

Origen. *Against Celsus*.

Oxford Dictionaries. Internet. Available from http://www.oxforddictionaries.com/us/definition/american_english/flourish, accessed May 8, 2014.

"Urban Population." *The Henry J. Kaiser Family Foundation*. Internet. Available from http://kff.org/global-indicator/urban-population/, accessed May 8, 2014.

THE PROSPERITY GOSPEL'S TRANSFORMATION OF THE POPULAR RELIGIOUS IMAGINATION

KATE BOWLER

Flourish. It is one of those splashy seminary words popularized in the 21st century as Catholics and mainline Protestants in particular attempted to grapple with appropriate theological language for a God of more. All of a sudden "human flourishing," individual and communal, was at the center of theological encounters with everything from pastoral care to medicine, education, psychology, human rights and environmental science. Embedded in the sweeping effort to fathom the preconditions of flourishing was the sheer scarcity of appropriate alternatives: abundance, prosperity, success or happiness all seemed too individualistic, too shallow or too economic. Lingering too was the fear that the Christian world was awash with maximalist language of more and better that made the American Dream seemingly interchangeable with the Good Life. They were right.

When the pastor of America's largest church, Joel Osteen, sits down with the ladies from the hit talk show "The View," audiences love his squinting smile and drawling confidence that God provides the tools to reach into the heavenlies and pull out a blessing: a promotion, weight loss, a lovely home, a happy marriage or top-flight schools for their kids. Osteen's book titles said it all: *Your Best Life Now, It's Your Time,* and *Every Day a Friday.* Over the last 50 years, North Americans have been witness to a transformation in the popular religious imagination about the appreciable differences that faith in God can make. An average American attending one of the country's largest megachurches, tuning in to any major Christian television stations, or picking up a cheap paperback at Walmart has a very high probability of learning a new vocabulary. They will learn how to "release" their faith, to use their minds to achieve their desires, or to believe God "for" something as they put their contributions in the offertory plate. They will sing its praises with the latest contemporary Christian music not realizing that they are deep into a Hillsong chorus springing from Australia's largest prosperity megachurch. The prosperity gospel is simultaneously everywhere and nowhere because it sounds so sweet and so familiar.

The prosperity gospel is an offshoot of pentecostalism that centers on a new understanding of faith. Faith, rather than simple trust, is re-imagined as a spiritual power released by positive thoughts and words. This faith-formula was a blend of early 20th-century American theologies of self-help, popular psychology, metaphysical philosophy and can-do attitudes about the power of the mind. But it was not always so mainstream. In the 1940s and 1950s, when pentecostal denominations began to build their own mighty institutions and confidence in their place in American society, some began to yearn for the untamed signs and wonders of its earliest days. Ministers began to break off on their own to tour the country as miracle workers, evangelists, and especially healers, setting up make-shift canvas sanctuaries for a few nights at stops in towns and cities across Canada and the United States.[1] These tent-toting pentecostal healers like Oral Roberts, Kenneth Hagin and A. A. Allen expanded on earlier radical evangelical theologies about what the power of faith could do. By their teaching and their example, they showed a generation of believers how they could wield their faith to change their circumstances. Faith could heal bodies, multiply finances, restore families and bring a taste of heaven down to earth. Some were brash and controversial like A. A. Allen, known for his claims of miraculous oil exuding from participants' foreheads or billfolds that multiplied money tucked into it. Others were winsome and affable like Oral Roberts, who rolled up his sleeves and won audiences' hearts with his willingness to say that all aspects of people's lives were precious in God's sight. People turned to these ministers with prayer requests for everything from jobs to cancer remission to a hankering for a new Chevrolet.[2] An emergent "prosperity gospel," which is to say belief the power of positive faith spoken aloud to achieve health, wealth, and victory, was beginning to gain credibility and focus.

These pentecostal outsiders, often from the wrong side of the tracks, might never have achieved a lasting platform had it not been for the cresting of another revival, this time among the disaffected young and the white middle-class. It would be called for the 'charismatic movement' for it fanned the flames of spiritual gifts, particularly speaking in tongues, that were once only pentecostal domain. Catholic and mainline Protestant audiences began to experiment with pentecostal theologies of spiritual power and heady gifts of the spirit, bridging old divides that allowed the emerging prosperity gospel to reach beyond pentecostals to new enthusiastic audiences.

By the 1970s the prosperity gospel could be heard seven days a week by a host of smiling preachers at the helm of sprawling Christian television empires. Though

---

1. David Edwin Harrell, *All Things Are Possible: The Healing and Charismatic Revivals in Modern America* (Bloomington: Indiana University Press, 1979).

2. For a testimony thanking God for faith that brought him a new Lincoln Continental, see Gene Ewing, *A Miracle For You* (Fort Worth, TX: Campmeeting Revivals Inc., 1964), 16.

its ministers dubbed it "old-time religion," the movement had been remade from a Holy Ghost revival into a confident network of megachurches, popular conferences, ministerial associations, and Bible schools scattered across denominations and independent churches. It was becoming a household faith for white, black and Hispanic America, garnering wide audiences as it saturated radio and television, inspirational paperbacks, and the pulpits of large congregations springing up across the suburban Sunbelt. With T. L and Daisy Osborn lounging in leisure suits in their *National Enquirer* advertisements and Oral Roberts's television specials attracting audiences on par with the Macy's Day parade, the prosperity gospel had clearly made a comfortable home in American culture.

Theologically pentecostal and ecclesially independent, the prosperity gospel typically centered on four themes: faith, wealth, health, and victory.[3] Faith, spoken aloud, loosed spiritual forces. Its evangelists developed an understanding of faith as a tool to activate spiritual power that drew blessings into the believer's life. Ministers like Fred Price and soon Creflo Dollar, Eddie Long and T.D. Jakes would bring variations of the prosperity gospel to black religious programming by the 1980s and early 1990s, while Guillermo Maldonado, Alberto Delgado and Marcos Witt popularized Latino prosperity gospels drawn from immigrant and Anglo networks a decade later. Christianity soared with visions of what right-believing and right-speaking believers could accomplish.

The significance of the rise of the prosperity gospel for Christian community development lies not so much in the particular sectarian history I have outlined but in the blurriness around the movement itself. When I first began my study almost a decade ago, I attended a local prosperity megachurch and was baffled by its completely disavowal of any history, movement or connection between itself and any other church. They seemed like a sea of solo evangelists with a label that was too slippery to pin down. After all, no one wants to be called a "prosperity preacher." Just ask Joel Osteen who just sat down recently with the Huffington Post to tell Americans (again) why he shouldn't count as one with the addition of his new SiriusXM channel to his media empire.

But the indistinct boundaries around what constitutes the "prosperity gospel" and what does not is, in fact, its greatest achievement. It was hard to tell the difference between a Joel Osteen and an Oprah and Donald Trump when it came to their faith that good people always end up on top. Every celebrity, religious or not, seemed to agree that there was no such thing as luck.

By the 21st century, the prosperity gospel was synonymous with a Christianity that people could put into action. Its preachers doubled as therapists, able to tease out the spiritual significance of a tangled thought world. T.D. Jakes made regular

---

3. Kate Bowler, *Blessed: A History of the American Prosperity Gospel* (New York: Oxford University Press, 2013). See chapter 2 for "faith," chapter 3 for "wealth," chapter 4 for "health," and chapter 5 for "victory."

appearances on the country's favorite therapy talk show, Dr. Phil, as a fellow expert in the human heart and mind. Men and women at work who wanted a little spiritual insight downloaded their podcasts in record numbers, particularly the host middle-aged women who wanted to hear Joyce Meyer's latest on positivity and emotional discipline. Elderly ladies sitting at home tuned in to wall-to-wall prosperity theology as it blanketed TBN, CBN, Daystar, and local channels as the most watched religious programs in the nation. A recent Time poll found that 17 percent of Christians surveyed identified themselves as part of this movement, while 31 percent believed that God increases the riches of those who give. A later Pew survey reported that 43 percent of all Christian respondents agreed that the faithful receive health and wealth.[4]

The modern success story of the prosperity gospel is the story of how millions of Americans came to believe in its vision of "soft prosperity." Soft prosperity is a phrase I coined to explain the theological correlation between positive words and attitudes with a positive result. It is the kind of bumper sticker theology that is perfectly captured by the old slogans of Oral Roberts campaigns, like "God is a good God!," "Expect a Miracle!" or "Something good is going to happen to you!" It is vague, catchy, and assured. Soft prosperity rose to fame after the 'hard prosperity' of 1980s televangelism became associated with greed and weeping preachers. Hard prosperity favors mechanistic language that plots a direct link between faith and circumstances, as in someone who refuses to voice a medical diagnosis for fear the negative words will cause it to happen. Its softer counterpart rose to popularity in the 1990s with the turn toward therapeutic religion and the desire for language of sweet certainty. It was the perfect theological language for an experiential and consumptive generation who longed for a God who not only showed up but whose blessings could be measured.

Any account of flourishing must take stock of a popular religious imagination captivated by this new Christian empiricism with its guarantees of measurable improvements. Recent evangelical overtures into tithing as "God's system" backed by the church's money-back guarantee (to ensure tithes are supernaturally repaid supernaturally in 90 days) is suggestive of the deep pull of results-based religion. White evangelicalism, in particular, is the new frontier for the prosperity gospel as a reflection of its increasingly therapeutic and sunny certainty that sanctification can be plotted as ceaseless growth. Though megachurch evangelicals like Rick Warren and Bill Hybels continued to decry the prosperity gospel, others slipped an arm around Joel Osteen and encouraged their members to get blessed. Every hardship was a trial or a lesson, and every obstacle an opportunity to foretell a brighter future. Religiously speaking, it was no longer acceptable to sing the blues. Celebratory rejoinders of "I'm blessed" and "God is good . . . all the time!" have drifted from Sunday mornings to become the part of a reflexive chit chat of causal encounter. Those phrases, to be sure, have a long history particularly in African American communities of sharing accounts of

---

4. David Van Biema and Jeff Chu, "Does God Want You To Be Rich?," *Time*, Internet, available from http://www.time.com/time/magazine/article/0,9171,1533448,00.html, accessed January 7, 2010.

faithfulness. But the new priority of positive affect suggests a wider cultural priority of perpetual happiness that is transforming our vocabulary of gratitude. The challenge for Christian communities devoted to the transformation of whole communities is to maintain language layered with the ability to lament and praise, tear down as well as build up, or even to decline without a steady plan for the way forward.

Prosperity preachers adore Jeremiah 29 for its promise to prosper God's people and offer them hope. But the careful observer of prosperity theology and this new turn in popular religion will note that Christian communities are no longer simply offering hope—they peddle certainty. Kenneth Hagin, often (mistakenly) credited as founding the prosperity movement, was famous for his vision of faith as a spiritual law could operate with the predictability of gravity. Faith was a true guarantee. Every prayer went answered. Every donation was repaid. Every doctor revoked the diagnosis that foretold an early end. The dignity embedded in the prosperity gospel lay in its ability to reach into all areas of life and call it God's business. It is in this account of the good life that the world of Christian community development finds traction, for it too is a story about human flourishing that casts a vision of God reaching into the mundane. It is a story not just about salvation, justification and sanctification but of the high price of utilities, the educational future of an errant child or the quality of care for a mother worried about a lump in her breast. It shares the prosperity gospel's totalizing account of a universe in which all aspects of life count as significant to the body of Christ. The idea of the secular, the mundane or the ordinary simply vanishes. These accounts of more, better, abundance and flourishing are ultimately language of spiritual forecasting that peek into the future and report back, competing promises and guarantees that the faithful long to hear where, in some form or fashion, God desires to bless them.

BIBLIOGRAPHY

Biema, David Van and Jeff Chu. "Does God Want You To Be Rich?." *Time*. Internet. Available from http://www.time.com/time/magazine/article/0,9171,1533448,00.html, accessed January 7, 2010.

Bowler, Kate. *Blessed: A History of the American Prosperity Gospel*. New York: Oxford University Press, 2013.

Ewing, Gene. *A Miracle For You*. Fort Worth, TX: Campmeeting Revivals Inc., 1964.

Harrell, David Edwin. *All Things Are Possible: The Healing and Charismatic Revivals in Modern America*. Bloomington: Indiana University Press, 1979.

OGBU KALU, AFRICAN PENTECOSTALISM AND SHALOM

VALERIE LANDFAIR

This article examines a re-visioning of an African worldview of shalom in conversation with some of the tenets within the Prosperity Gospel. Specifically, I propose a theology of shalom in African Pentecostalism through the readings of Ogbu Kalu in conversation with the Prosperity Gospel. I explore the resonance between the Bible and African indigenous worldview. Due to the multitudes of nations in Africa and her complex cultures, innumerable languages and religions, I will examine Ghana as a case study.

My interest arises out of a conversation with one of my peers, an Anglo male divinity student, who asked, "why do African American and African churches talk so much about money?" I immediately performed an impromptu interview and discovered he was a third generation college educated individual who went on yearly family vacations to his grandparent's cottage. He grew up in a church where mission excursions were normative and he was a recipient of medical and health plans. The task of exposing, naming, and calling sinners to repentance for a theology focused only on wealth, power, and glory is in tension with a theology that poverty and suffering builds character and your mansion awaits you on the other side - heaven.

Pentecostalism in Africa

The Prosperity Gospel or the Word of Faith Gospel in Africa has attracted millions of poor and middle class Christians within the Pentecostal movement. In Nigeria the Canaanland Church in Lagos seats over 55,000 people weekly and the church is part of the 5,000-acre complex.[1] Redeemed Christian Church of God attracts 300,000 people

---

1. *David Oyedepo Ministries International Incorporated*, Internet, available from http://www3.davidoyedepoministries.org, accessed July 21, 2014.

with churches in over 150 countries of the world.[2] Criticisms of outlandish material-ism, private airplanes, fancy cars and expansive mansions reverberate throughout the academy, airwaves, and blogs. However, this movement has established the largest church complexes in the world consisting of the church, schools, medical facilities, orphanages, as well as sponsoring African missionaries to spread the word of Christ in the United States.

The growth of Christianity in Africa and particularly Pentecostal, Charismatic and Neo-Pentecostal Christianity should not be viewed uncritically. Critique of Gha-naian Prosperity Theology should balance the good being done by the Holy Spirit in the growth of the church with the corruption in wealth distribution and taking another's possessions or property for personal gain. One can argue that the good is seen in the souls that are being saved and the ministries that are flourishing.

How one understands God affects the way one understands and lives out one's be-lief. Theology tends to be historically and culturally determined. The context in which theology develops plays a formative role in how one applies and interprets God's word in life. In Africa, the intersection of culture and theology addresses concerns related to wholeness and empowerment. It seems to be a common misconception that African Christianity and especially African Pentecostalism are exports from North America and the Western world. Allan Anderson assumes "that most Spirit-type churches in Southern Africa owe their origins" to William J. Seymour and John Alexander Dowie.[3] Anderson's conclusions negate the testimony of Scripture that God's Spirit has moved, is moving, and continues to move throughout the nations. The praise "the earth is the Lord's, and everything in it, the world, and all who live in it" includes spirit-filled-Pentecostal-Africa.[4] The complexity and fluidity of this historical discourse is out-lined in Ogbu Kalu's *An Introduction to African Pentecostalism,* which examines the charismatic revivals in the colonial period, 1900–1960, independence era, and from 1907–2000.[5] From this perspective, Kalu views Ethiopianism and the prophet move-ments as the historical roots of African Pentecostalism.

In the historical revivals in Africa, Pentecostalism resonated with Africans' "power theme in indigenous religions, the power that sustained the cosmos, the so-cioeconomic and political structures, the power that gave meaning to life's journey, . . . and the sojourn in the ancestral world."[6] Kalu argues that African revivals are con-cerned with spiritual, economic, political, and structures of power. Kenneth Archer affirms Kalu's position, "God is a living, dynamic, personal being who can presently

2. *Redeemed Christian Church of God,* Internet, available from https://trccg.org/rccg/, accessed July 21, 2014.

3. Allan Anderson, *Moya: The Holy Spirit in an African Context* (Pretoria, South Africa: Univer-sity of South Africa, 1991), 26.

4. Psalm 24:1 (New International Standard)

5. Ogbu Kalu, *African Pentecostalism* (Oxford: Oxford University Press, 2008), 3.

6. Ibid., 4.

intervene and change situations dramatically."[7] Pentecostal ethos took seriously people's need for power to overcome their fear of spirit forces, colonization, principalities, racism, demons, classism, and witches. God's spiritual powers are appropriated to bring deliverance and restoration to communities and individuals from 'all' afflictions of witchcraft, ancestral curses and evil spirits.

Traditional African Religions that embodies Africans' quest for power and identity find similar spiritual expressions within Pentecostal, African Independent Churches, and the practices of Islam. African Pentecostalism stresses that because Africans are God's people, "people of the covenant," the covenantal agreements grant access to a personal relationship with the powerful triune God. As a covenant partner of God, Africans are a people defined by obedience. The covenantal relationships allow Africans to place a demand on the love and faithfulness of "God and God's Word" for immediate visible manifestations of God's power by God's Spirit.

Kalu contends that Pentecostalism and Islam "became birds of the same feather by opposing modernity and stressing the inerrancy of their respective canons, nationalism, opposition to modernity, minority consciousness."[8] Both claim "authentic expression of their respective traditions' place stress on distinctive elements, activism, moralistic puritan ethics, . . . disagree with the supremacy of reason over revelation; de-emphasis of the supernatural, and the permitting of relativistic, universalistic ethics."[9] The two religions differ in regards to God, covenant, prayer, charisma, religious experiences and what they see as sacred text.[10]

Hebrew Ancestors

Clifton Clarke argues that the Old Testament resonates with the African outlook on life.[11] Thomas Oduro believes that the experiences of the children of God in the Old Testament mirrored the experiences of Africans. Various indigenous religious motifs "have regulated the lives of many Africans for many years. Most of them were, however, suppressed in many of the churches established by the Western missionaries.[12]

7. Kenneth Archer, *The Gospel Revisited: Towards a Pentecostal Theology* (Eugene, Oregon: Pickwick, 2010), 86.

8. Kalu, *African Pentecostalism*, 251.

9. Ibid., 251–52.

10. Ibid., 254.

11. Clifton R. Clarke, *African Christology* (Eugene, OR: Pickwick, 2011), 47.

12. Thomas Oduro, "A Brief Introduction of African Independent Churches," Lutheran University Press (2007): 19. Oduro cites: "blood sacrifices (particularly human blood), seeing visions and dreaming, the building and use of altars, the importance of priests and shrines, undertaking of pilgrimages, defined domestic roles of husbands, wives, and children, mode of training children, types of marriages – monogamy and polygamy, belief in and veneration of ancestors, the use of herbs and other natural elements as agents of healing, belief in miracles, the importance of fecundation in marriage, belief in angels as messengers of deities, dietary regulations as vehicles of holiness, rituals and many other concepts."

Bible translation into African languages enabled the African Christian to distinguish the continuity with their Hebrew ancestors. Africans deduced that they held more in common with "Holy Scripture" than the Scriptures taught by the missionaries. Clarke concludes, "Scripture translated into the vernacular became an independent standard of reference, and it soon became apparent that much of what was taught by missionaries was more a reflection of their own cultural baggage than from the Bible.[13]

One's ability to read scripture and hear God speak to them in their native tongues affirmed their experiences that God sees the people of Africa as worthy to receive divine power and encounters. A common sermon theme within the Prosperity Gospel is that the blessings of Abraham are for Abraham's descendants and the good news is that the blessing is also poured out upon people of color in Africa, Asia, and Latin America. Africans see their oral and written stories intersecting throughout the Hebrew's narratives affirming "God communicating with "our ancestors" in history through "various ways, means, and people."[14]

Anderson contends that people have a need for power when they feel powerless. In African pre-Christian religions, God as the ultimate cause of creation is the absolute source of all power.[15] To the African, God's powers are not restricted to the Old Testament covenant, but to a more powerful covenant with better promises made two thousand years ago "fully fulfilled in the coming, life, death, and resurrection of Jesus Christ."[16] The evidence of their covenantal agreement sealed with the baptism of the Holy Spirit testifies that "not only white people could be great and powerful, but also a mighty one, a man worthy of note, could as well arise from the rank of Africans, whom the Europeans scorned."[17] Kalu contends that the prosperity movements' theology is located in Jesus and Scripture by "acting on the word, speaking into reality what does not exist, and dreaming and envisioning the desired goals."[18]

Shalom Theology

Shalom is a covenantal theology of wholeness. Jesus is concerned with the fullness of Africa's salvation, the "total wholeness that is physical, psychological, spiritual and

13. Clifton R. Clarke, *African Christology: Jesus in Post-Missionary African Christianity* (Eugene, OR: Pickwick, 2011), 47.

14. Agbonkhianmeghe E. Orobator, *Theology Brewed in an African Pot* (Maryknoll, NY: Orbis, 2008), 15.

15. Allan Anderson, "African Initiated Churches of the Spirit and Pneumatology," *Word & World* 23, (2003): 183.

16. Orobator, *Theology Brewed*, 16.

17. Emmanuel Martey, "Prophetic Movements in the Congo: The Life and Work of Simon Kimbangu and How His Followers Saw Him," *Journal of African Instituted Church Theology* 1, (2006): 9.

18. Kalu, *African Pentecostalism*, 261.

social. . . . Prosperity theology, therefore, emerges from covenant theology, the concept of salvation, and the atoning death of Christ."[19]

Ghana's "new church" has embraced the global prosperity movements' basic theology.[20] However, African prosperity movement also captures the voice of a people, whom European society has often labeled 'unlovable'. African Christians are transforming the imported prosperity movements to cope with economic, political and social changes. This allows the followers of the prosperity movement to reject old modes of Christian expression, particularly regarding the issue of poverty. This conversion of the 'traditional missionary gospel' allows African Christians to have a vision, place, and identity within a larger section of society outside of their community. They are given language to reframe their own experiences of poverty and suffering from a permanent location to a temporal position. God's desire to heal, prosper, and shower blessings are appeals that resonate across social class and religious denominations. Many African communities share the understanding that prosperity and wealth are not material, but reflect inner peace, satisfaction, contentment, and the maintenance of social networks.[21]

David Tonghou rightly critiques the prosperity gospel themes embedded in some forms of African Pentecostalism in the "inordinate stress on the miraculous" to heal, deliver, and bless. One is torn between the good being done and the corruption. Faith and hope are the byproducts that are being birthed within African communities that God can heal, deliver, and bless one's labor.[22] Tonghou argues that this spiritualized ethos of empowerment has actually undermined human flourishing in Africa by redirecting the passion for the Kingdom of God from regarding the establishment of government infrastructure to tackle social justices, HIV, socio-economic services, and the divine inspiration of the scientific and technology imaginations.[23] Tonghou believes that the tenets have shifted the teaching of love, liberation, and empowerment of "life" to a Spirit baptism of personal well-being and self-seeking activities.[24]

Prosperity teaching and prayer are a way of appropriating Scripture to prophetically identify and dismantle the disharmony in Africa and construct shalom. Kalu argues that because of Africans' understanding of covenant agreements given in the Old Testament, African Pentecostalism accepts the causality of poverty within the Old Testament: "the oppression of the rich, religious apostasy, social alienation, ecological causes, human factors, and self-alienation or lifestyle." The Old Testament's

19. Ibid., 261.

20. Paul Gifford, *Ghana's New Christianity: Pentecostalism in a Globalizing African Economy* (Bloomington, Indiana: Indiana University Press, 2004), 44.

21. Kalu, *African Pentecostalism*, 261.

22. David Tonghou Ngong, *The Holy Spirit and Salvation in African Christian Theology: Imagining a More Hopeful Future for Africa* (New York: Peter Lang, 2010), 128.

23. Ibid., 140.

24. Ibid., 134.

diagnosis of poverty draws a distinction between external, internal, and moral causes. Individual responsibility is still as essential as the external causes.

Poverty is linked to rebellion against God's will, sabbath-breaking, failure to tithe, bad governance, bureaucratic and fiscal irresponsibility, famine, drought, hurricanes, plagues, death, illness, poor sanitation, agricultural practices, the depletion of natural resources, laziness, disobedience to parents, immorality, and sexual orientation.[25] The appropriation of prosperity teaching and preaching for Africans is a poverty-alleviation strategy that includes spiritual warfare prayers aimed at curing the disharmony through prayer and fasting, resocialization, and renewal of consciousness.[26] In appropriating prayer as spiritual warfare, the evil forces and spirits are eradicated in villages, towns, cities, and nations. Onwona states that "there are strongholds of greed, lust, seduction, Jezebel, sexual immorality, hatred, envy, jealousy, corruption, witchcraft, and sorcery" tools of the "devil's establishment for propagating evil and unrighteousness."[27] Onwona's statement leads one to ponder on the tension between God and individual responsibility regarding the eradication of evil spirits. Ngong believes that this type of prayer tends to discredit the advancement of Africa, while endorsing an African spiritual cosmology ethos of prophecy, healing, deliverance, and protection against evil spirits, which perpetrates capitalistic greed by widening the gap between the rich and the poor.[28]

The Ghanaian Akan resonates with the Hebrew concept of shalom, denoting total wholeness that is physical, psychological, spiritual, and social. For the African, it describes peace with God, the gods, ancestors, fellow human beings (family and community), and the natural world. Emmanuel Martey has pointed out, "At the individual level, the African believes God rescues him or her from dangers of sickness, witchcraft, sorcery, magic, barrenness, misfortune, troublesome spirits, calamity, failure and death. At the community level, rescue comes from such dangers as drought, war, oppression, foreign domination, slavery, locust invasion, epidemic, floods and so on."[29] The concept of shalom includes individual salvation and liberation of African community from all oppressions. One discerns that the roots of shalom are anchored in God's authority, God's covenant, that God has dominion over everything and, hence, the right to give it to whoever He pleases."[30]

Paul Gifford observes a new Christianity in Ghana that emphasizes teaching and prayers on economic victory and success. Victory for overall healing is stressed over physical healing. Conversations regarding the last days are focused on restoration

25. Kalu, *African Pentecostalism*, 257.

26. Ibid., 258.

27. Samuel Ofori Onwona, *Shadows Come to Light: Prayer as Spiritual Warfare* (Achimota, Ghana: Africa Christian Press, 2000), 17.

28. Ngong, *Holy Spirit*, 8.

29. Martey, "Prophetic Movements," 9.

30. Onwona, *Shadows Come*, 17.

impulses instead of soul winning.[31] Kalu affirms the capacity of African Pentecostal prosperity theology "to re-imagine the gospel from an indigenous idiom. Pentecostal theology does not encourage the people to fold their arms and wait for manna to drop from the skies: rather, poverty-alleviation strategies in indigenous communities are far more nuanced."[32] Clarke states that the Pentecostal ethos "brought an appropriation of the gospel message where it was now possible to experience the power of Christ" and that the power of Christ could operate without limits or boundaries in the African worldview.[33]

The Christ of Pentecost healed the sick, cast out demons, raised the dead and gave food to the poor and needy. Clarke states that the effect of the prosperity message on the African "extended beyond the cosmic powers of Christ to bring healing and wholeness and added a social and financial element of health and wealth that could also be accessed through the domain of spiritual breakthroughs."[34] Might one interpret the prosperity message as teaching the "full" gospel, grounded in the teaching of the Old and New Testaments "that salvation is essentially freedom from sickness and affliction of all kinds and the agents that bear them? This understanding of healing and wholeness therefore goes beyond symptomatic healing" to also address the casual factors.[35]

African Pentecostalism affirms that "prayer is a primary means to moving the hand of God."[36] The spiritual worldview of the African encompasses all of creation, surrounded by spiritual entities that are more powerful and could be malevolent. This worldview, coupled with the internal and external demonic forces of disharmony call for a daily dependence on God for the African to living peacefully in such a world.[37] Consequently, Africans tend to pray about almost everything and everyone. Prayer services are held every Sunday morning, during the weekday, during national holidays, and mid-morning in churches. Africans pray in homes, community centers, businesses, schools, prayer-mountains, and government buildings. Chris Oyakhilome contends "certain prayer sessions are specially designed by the Lord to help straighten out things in the spirit-realm."[38] Kalu argues, "Pentecostals perceive themselves as the beneficiaries of increasing revelations of divine wisdom and resources" in prayer.[39]

31. Gifford, *Ghana's New Christianity*, 80–82.

32. Kalu, *African Pentecostalism*, 260.

33. Clarke, *African Christology*, 65.

34. Ibid., 66.

35. Ibid., 124.

36. Thomas Oduro, "Prayer and Ritual in African Spirituality," Unpublished, Accra, Ghana, (2010): 3.

37. Ibid., 4.

38. Chris Oyakhilome, *How to Pray Effectively Volume One* (South Africa: LoveWorld Publishing Ministry, 2012), 7.

39. Kalu, *African Pentecostalism*, 250.

Prosperity theology emphasizes that God's promised generosity, as demonstrated with Abraham, is available for every believing Christian on earth today. The African worldview consists of covenantal imagery and language, therefore, they embrace teachings and prayers regarding legal and spiritual contract. Each believer has the ability to access it, claim it, and possess it.[40] One genre of the African Prosperity message focuses on how faith shapes prayer and how different types of prayers should be used to access different types of prosperity; therefore, using the wrong tool for the wrong purpose courts failure. Prayers of faith, prayers of agreement, intercessory prayer, prayers of dedication, and anointing are only efficacious when used appropriately to access the blessings once promised to Abraham. Another part of the Prosperity Gospel teaches that one must invest before reaping any dividends; that one must sow before harvesting. The quantity of harvest is a function of the size of acreage cultivated, so believers sow tithes and offerings.[41] One understands how this teaching undermines God's grace.

Pentecostalism represents a paradigm shift that unshackles theology from rationalistic, scientific ways of thinking and expands the understanding of the spiritual dimensions of reality and the operations of the invisible world. It posits that there are three different ways of knowing—intellectual, observational, and experience—and accords new emphasis to the realm of human experience. It says that the power of the Scriptures does not reside in the letter; rather, God is behind the law.[42] Amos Yong argues "the Pentecostal experience of the Spirit is the experience of the transformation of lives and communities as confronted by the living God."[43] Yong believes a Pentecostal doctrine of salvation leads to a pneumatological soteriology framework: centered on Jesus Christ and enabled by the Holy Spirit; dynamic, featuring distinctive experiences (e.g. repentance and baptism) yet set within a broader process; including theological (the forgiveness of sins) and social/intergenerational (children) dimensions; historical and social (the promise for Jews and those Gentiles "far away"); and involves human response (repentance) to divine initiative (God's call).[44]

Yong argues that a Pentecostal framework is in contrast to Protestant soteriology, which tends to bifurcate the work of Christ and of the Spirit. He constructs a Pentecostal pneumatological soteriology that understands salvation to be the work of both Christ and the Spirit from beginning to the end.[45] Yong argues that the historical saving work of the Spirit of God is holistic and multidimensional comprised of

40. Ibid., 255.

41. Kalu, *African Pentecostalism*, 255–56.

42. Ibid., 250.

43. Amos Yong, *The Spirit Poured Out on All Flesh: Pentecostalism and the Possibility of Global Theology* (Grand Rapids, MI: Baker Academic, 2005), 81.

44. Ibid., 82.

45. Ibid.

personal, familial, ecclesial, material, social, cosmic, and eschatological terms.[46] Is this not shalom?

Kalu's re-visioning of a shalom for Africa takes seriously the intersection between culture and theology and offers a critique of the past violence of colonization, slavery, systematic racism, sexism and classism as well as the current structures and systems that daily impede a theology of wholeness. By embedding one's identity in the personhood of Jesus, and by being empowered by one's Spirit baptism, one may rightly discern and appropriate narratives of empowerment by the Spirit regardless of race and class. I recognize that my Anglo male divinity peer might continue to lump and dismiss African and African American teachings regarding money, health, peace, welfare, safety, soundness, tranquility, and prosperity to be foolishness of the Pentecostal movements, thereby overlooking or silencing the prophetic voices of hope and protest against unjust societal structures, systems, and practices, both within and outside of the Universal Church.

In conclusion, Ogbu Kalu's African Pentecostalism reconstructs an African worldview of shalom containing covenant imagery and language, connection with Biblical ancestors, spiritual prayers, and reconstructing a theology that reclaims the prosperity message of shalom for Africa.[47] Shalom is understood as the harmony within a new world for this generation of empowered spirit-filled Africans. The genius of the pneumatological soteriology is found in appropriation of the full gospel promises and curses within God's covenantal agreement: a covenant that grants access through prayer for a demand on God's word. The power of God transferred to the people of God in Africa to reconstruct an African Christianity worldview of *Shalom for Africa*.

BIBLIOGRAPHY

Anderson, Allan. "African Initiated Churches of the Spirit and Pneumatology." *Word & World* 23, (2003): 178–86.

_____. *Moya: The Holy Spirit in an African Context*. Pretoria, South Africa: University of South Africa, 1991.

Archer, Kenneth. *The Gospel Revisited: Towards a Pentecostal Theology*. Eugene, OR: Pickwick, 2010.

Clarke, Clifton R. *African Christology: Jesus in Post-Missionary African Christianity*. Eugene, OR: Pickwick, 2011.

Gifford, Paul. *Ghana's New Christianity: Pentecostalism in a Globalizing African Economy*. Bloomington, IN: Indiana University Press, 2004.

Kalu, Ogbu. *African Pentecostalism: An Introduction*. Oxford: Oxford University Press, 2008.

_____. *African Christianity: An African Story*. Trenton, NJ: African World Press, 2007.

Martey, Emmanuel. "Prophetic Movements in the Congo: The Life and Work of Simon Kimbangu and How His Followers Saw Him." *Journal of African Instituted Church Theology* 1, (2006):1–16.

46. Ibid., 117–118.

47. Kalu, *African Pentecostalism*, 178–179.

Ngong, David Tonghou. *The Holy Spirit and Salvation in African Christian Theology: Imagining a More Hopeful Future for Africa.* New York: Peter Lang, 2010.

Oduro, Thomas. "A Brief Introduction of African Independent Churches." Lutheran University Press, (2007): 2–35.

_____. "Prayer and Ritual in African Spirituality: The Perspective of African Independent Churches." Unpublished, Accra, Ghana, (2010): 1- 15.

Onwona, Samuel Ofori. *Shadows Come to Light: Prayer as Spiritual Warfare.* Achimota, Ghana: Africa Christian Press, 2000.

Orobator, Agbonkhianmeghe E. *Theology Brewed In An African Pot.* Maryknoll, NY: Orbis, 2008.

Oyakhilome, Chris. *How to Pray Effectively.* South Africa: LoveWorld Publishing Ministry, 2012.

Yong, Amos. *The Spirit Poured Out on All Flesh: Pentecostalism and the Possibility of Global Theology.* Grand Rapids, MI: Baker Academic, 2005.

CITIES OF GOD: RECLAIMING CULTURE THROUGH THE FLOURISHING OF THE CITY

ALLIE WONG

"New York is great but I could *never* live there," is a common sentiment to hear from those who have passed through the city. They marvel at the way a frenetic Times Square at midnight can shine like the afternoon sun, and then they retreat to their quiet lives where no one is asking if you have any spare change or elbowing you out of the way to rush to work. While I understand this perspective and by no means believe urban living is for everyone, I wrestle with how to respond to the consumeristic platitudes that pervade such significant cities as New York—transitory homes to many who would take the opportunities city life has to offer before settling down where it is more "realistic" or "comfortable" to nest. Such transience is not uncharacteristic of Christians and occurs just as often within the Church as it does outside of it. Yet cultural transformation is bound up with the city. If the Church has any hope of thriving amidst an ever-secularizing culture,[1] it is vital for us to consider how to live, work and play strategically for the purposes of the Gospel.

A few years back while fundraising to go into full-time ministry in New York City, I hate to admit that I capitalized on the Church's often-hackneyed vilification of the city at large: a place of godlessness and rebellion where sin was rampant and lost people in need of someone—namely *me*—to direct them to a nice, moral life. While some of these attributes hold some weight, they are no less true of the suburbs, nor are they the full story of what *is* true of the city—a mosaic paradox of culture where sacred and profane fuse together in the beautifully gritty faces of human brokenness and human flourishing. The city has historically been a symbol of progress and a catalyst for culture, industry and power. The magnitude of its influence, however, has never been as significant as it is at this moment in human history. In a recent study of global

---

1. "The number of Americans who do not identify in surveys with any religion—the "nones"—has been growing at a dramatic pace. As of 2012, one-fifth of the US public—and a third of adults under 30—were religiously unaffiliated, the highest percentages ever in Pew Research Center polling." Paul Taylor and the Pew Research Center, *The Next America* (New York: PublicAffairs, 2014), 127.

population expansion, the United Nations anticipates that by the year 2050 nearly 70% of the world's population will live in cities.[2] In a world of rapid globalization, technological advancement and a seemingly boundless public square, the exponential growth of cities is not only expanding in population but also in sphere of influence. Considering this reality, it is now more imperative than ever for the Church to prioritize city engagement as vital to its own posterity. "If the church in the West remains, for the most part, in suburbs of Middle America and neglects the great cities, it risks losing an entire generation of American society's leaders.[3]"

God's heart and purpose for the city is not unique to the 21st century West. In Jeremiah 29:7 God urges the exiled Israelites to "seek the peace and the prosperity"— the *shalom*, or wholeness—of the city. He also promises that the flourishing of his people would be in tandem with that of Babylon—the city in which they have found themselves captive. Though they clung to the hope and promise of his deliverance, the Israelites were charged by God to settle in Babylon and knit themselves into the literal and cultural landscape. The promise of future restoration and return was not intended to eclipse the importance of living in the present, fully engaged in the culture at hand. Through Jeremiah, God cautions the Israelites against living transiently and in cultural isolation:

> This is what the Lord Almighty, the God of Israel, says to all those I carried into exile from Jerusalem to Babylon: 'Build houses and settle down; plant gardens and eat what they produce. Marry and have sons and daughters; find wives for your sons and give your daughters in marriage, so that they too may have sons and daughters. Increase in number there; do not decrease. Also, seek the peace and prosperity of the city to which I have carried you into exile. Pray to the Lord for it, because if it prospers, you too will prosper. (Jeremiah 29: 4–7, NIV)

Jeremiah shows that God is calling his people to participate in cultural renewal of manifold wholeness, the message of which is still as relevant today as it was then. God's instruction was a four-fold holistic command that was and is the key to grasping the redemptive vision for the city and ultimately culture: (1) maintain an attitude of longevity through establishing residency, (2) become a part of the social and economic tapestry, (3) be literally and spiritually generational; and (4) flourish and thrive while doing 1–3.

Build houses and settle down. The first charge leads presumptuously with a certain degree of permanency: establish a geographical foundation in Babylon. For the Israelites, who were no strangers to wandering, what was countercultural in this mandate was to reject attitudes and actions of transiency. By consciously taking up residence in

---

2. "World Urbanization Prospects: The 2011 Revision," *The United Nations*, Department for Economic and Social Affairs, Internet, available from http://esa.un.org/unup/pdf/WUP2011_Highlights.pdf.

3. Timothy Keller, *Center Church* (Grand Rapids, MI: Zondervan, 2012), 160–161.

their place of captivity the Israelites were to reflect collective trust through an outward symbol of obedience. Similarly, if the 21st century Church is to be all things to all people we have to ask if where we live is strategic and what variables play the deciding role in where we locate.

Plant gardens and eat what they produce. As with any integration into an environment, the Israelites are being instructed to participate in local industry: to cultivate the land and partake in what it produces, to become a part of the agricultural and economic landscape in a way that contributes to systematic wellbeing. This disposition toward work has not deviated from what God expected of the Israelites, demonstrating that God's character is evidenced through God's people as they perform their work with integrity and excellence. Thus our work is reoriented from being about us to being a way to serve others and join God's purposes of cultivating.[4]

Marry and have sons and daughters in marriage so that they too may have sons and daughters. Increase in number; do not decrease. Echoing the first responsibility of humankind during Eden's unadulterated state,[5] God calls Israel to be fruitful and multiply. God's call is strategically and generationally to one of the most influential and powerful cities of the ancient world. Multiplication in this vein is indicative of flourishing and the emphasis on posterity is significant—God is urging Israel to not merely survive until eventual deliverance but to thrive in the place of captivity, being present to what is at hand. This idea is a radical shift from the idol of comfort and the consumeristic values that characterize modern America. Part of the risk that is being offered—both of the Israelites and of us today—is entrusting God with the wellbeing of one's family and community.

Seek the peace and prosperity of the city which I have carried you into exile—when it prospers you too will prosper. Finally, God goes so far as to unify the Israelites' ultimate wellbeing with that of their captors. While cultural and religious purity has historically been a primary value of the Israelites, the subtext of God's love for Babylon and the transcendent nature of the Gospel subverts the cultural, national, ethnic and even religious barriers innate to the Israelites' relationship to the Babylonians. God's word goes beyond a material or financial promise of comfort or wealth. Instead it is a "complete well-being, universal flourishing, wholeness, delight, and blessing . . .[this *shalom*] is a description of multidimensional wholeness and flourishing that is not just spiritual, but also material, physical, psychological, and economic.[6]"

Each of these components is indicative of a long-term view of cultural integration and cross-cultural sanctification. This call was unsettling considering that Israel had been promised their city, their land. And now they are called to reject the familiar and make their home in the city of their exile and, in effect, become a part of the

4. Ibid., 334.

5. Genesis 1:28

6. Stephen T. Um and Justin Buzzard, *Why Cities Matter: To God, the Culture, and the Church* (Wheaton, IL: Crossway, 2013), 88.

cultural fabric of their physical locale. While this charge was indeed radical, it was no less consistent with God's character than had been demonstrated even from the beginning in Eden.

Like the Israelites, the Church has been given the distinct call throughout the Biblical narrative to cultivate the Kingdom of God in the geographical contexts in which we find ourselves. As we consider the present-day implications of God's heart for the city, the question arises of what city flourishing translates to and how it is obtained. The prospering of a city, like that of an individual, means not only to grow and develop but also to do so with health, resilience and sustainability.[7]

Cities are historically places of ethnic, religious, economic and artistic diversity. Further they are microcosms of their nation or region. The Church must be integrated into every industry, life stage, culture and subculture that makes up the dynamic mosaic of humanity in city culture, reflecting the image of God with each varying facet. Thus the city must be comprehensively supplied with teachers, ministers, lawyers, actors, and investment bankers infusing their work and work-relationships with excellence and the character of Christ. The city, in all such complexities and coexisting variables, gives us glimpses of what heaven is intended to look like on earth. The climax of humanity occurs in Revelation 21 and 22 in the Holy City of God wherein all things are made new. The scene in Revelation 22 is a mirroring of Eden, a literal and figurative bookend upon which we see the entire Biblical meta-narrative consummated in the restoration of all things in the image of the garden city. This garden city contains Eden's familiar rivers and the Tree of Life, disentangled from the curse of sin. It is not arbitrary that the ultimate image of shalom is in a garden *city*.

The Language of the City:
Determining the Highest Value for Community Engagement

St. Augustine incisively noted that a people group is identified by the cherished things they hold in common.[8] While studying abroad in Prague during college I observed the term *genius loci*—Latin for *spirit of the place*—often tossed around in casual, academic and workplace environments as if the local anecdote were a universal reality. Those I engaged with often personified the city ascribing to it human like attributes, developing a personality and disposition from which one might build a relationship with the city itself. The term is derived from a common practice in ancient Rome wherein

---

7. Os Guinness observes, "A sustainable society is a self-renewing society in which, from generation to generation, the citizens choose to do what the society needs them to do if it is to last—in other words, a society in which leaders and citizens alike have cultivated habits of the heart to do without thinking what they need to do if they were to think about it. That is not happening in America today with freedom." Os Guinness, *A Free People's Suicide: Sustainable Freedom and the American Future* (Downers Grove, IL: InterVarsity Press, 2012), 34–35.

8. St. Augustine, *The City of God* (Peabody, MA: Hendrickson Publishers, 2009), Book19, Chapter 24.

symbols or totems representing the highest value or presiding ideal of a particular place served to stand guard or bless the thing on which it was ascribed. Such images as cornucopias to conjure prosperity, scales to uphold justice or libation bowls signifying piety were donned on everything from shrines to vases. Architectural theorist, Christian Norberg-Schulz describes: "This spirit gives life to people and places, accompanies them from birth to death, and determines their character. The *genius* thus corresponds to what a thing *is* or what it 'wants to be.'"[9]

Every city, as with every person, has a story and an ethos. Reading the tell-tale signs of our various places is the first threshold the Church must cross to begin developing the cultural intelligence needed to holistically engage the city in relevant Gospel dialogue. While such symbolism and incarnation as the Roman *genius loci* are not as overtly identifiable in contemporary American cities, there are still distinct indicators of what any given city's highest ideal is. What is the thing that is most cherished, the driving force, the thing that transcends the dividing walls of people groups or subcultures? Observing what people spend their time, money and energy on as well as observing the ways people garner respect, build relationships and uphold social rules are places to start. As Leonardo de Chirico describes:

> [There] are social idols that capture the life of the city . . . overarching sinful narratives on which people rely. We have to exegete them. We have to spot them out. We have to capture their core values, their history, their attractions, and the shape they have given to the city . . . We have to grasp spiritually the theological skyline of the city.[10]

The ethos of New York City, for example, in its rich history of immigration and the lofty promise of upward mobility touts the mantra by Frank Sinatra, made famous in his song "New York, New York": "If I can make it there, I'll make it anywhere." This fundamental ambition goes before the ruthless financer or aspiring Broadway actress as much as it does the undocumented immigrant and working poor. The *genius loci* of New York City's ambition is the unifying thread of most people groups regardless of economic, occupational, religious or ethnic identity. It is the theme woven through the city's history and the theme that continues to allure the next generation of New Yorkers.

What is essential is the development of cultural intelligence by way of learning to ask the right questions, becoming a keen observer, understanding how to engage with others, cultivate curiosity and share the Gospel in the language of the place. Discovering the highest value of a place is where we begin to unravel the heart of a people in order to translate the Gospel into a language that can be understood. It is paramount

9. Christian Norberg-Schulz, "Kahn, Heidegger and the Language of Architecture," *Oppositions* 18 (1979): 45.

10. Leonardo De Chirico, "Identifying the Idols of the City," *Q Ideas*, Internet, available from http://www.qideas.org/blog/identifying-the-idols-of-the-city.aspx/.

to not only identify the ethos of a city but also learn its language: "Until you understand your city's values, winsomely engaging it with the gospel of Jesus Christ will be a formidable task."[11]

We cannot afford to be negligent and turn a blind eye to the reality of the city as a place in need of the Body of Christ in ever-increasing measures; nor can we settle for the half-story, overlooking the beauty and image of our Creator hidden in the grit and the struggle. It is vital to think strategically about where we live, work and play and to resist gravitating toward that which is convenient, comfortable or even justifiably rational. This comes at no small cost, requiring our lives, our futures, our families, our dreams, supplanted by a vision for life-long development of a city and ultimately the world. As we yearn for ultimate restoration and cultural wholeness, it is essential that the Church's redemptive vision includes the city or it will remain fractured and incomplete. May we long to pursue the places colored by the collage of dreamers and vagabonds, shoebox apartments and penthouse suites, beauty and pain, high rollers and struggling artists. And in this pursuit, let us pray: His kingdom come to the city as it is in heaven.

BIBLIOGRAPHY

De Chirico, Leonardo. "Identifying the Idols of the City." *Q Ideas.* Internet. Available from http://www.qideas.org/blog/identifying-the-idols-of-the-city.aspx/.

Guinness, Os. *A Free People's Suicide: Sustainable Freedom and the American Future.* Downers Grove, IL: InterVarsity Press, 2012.

Keller, Timothy J. *Center Church: Doing Balanced, Gospel-centered Ministry in Your City.* Grand Rapids, MI: Zondervan, 2012.

Taylor, Paul and the Pew Research Center. *The Next America: Boomers, Millennials, and the Looming Generational Showdown.* New York, NY: PublicAffairs, 2014.

Um, Stephen T., and Justin Buzzard. *Why Cities Matter: To God, the Culture, and the Church.* Wheaton, IL: Crossway, 2013.

"World Urbanization Prospects: The 2011 Revision." *The United Nations.* Department for Economic and Social Affairs. Internet. Available from http://esa.un.org/unup/pdf/WUP2011_Highlights.pdf.

11. *Why Cities Matter*, 101.

FINDING OUR WAY HOME: WILL NEW URBANISM HELP THE CHURCH FIND ITS WAY BACK TO THE CITY?

SAMANTHA DOMINGO

Urban city centers undergoing extensive transformation related to the New Urbanism should cause the Church to reconsider ministry in terms of proximity, intentionality and practical theology. The possibility of reintegration into city centers throughout America creates motivation for churches to reenter the locations they once called home. How does the Church[1] begin to move towards reconciling themselves to the people and places that it intentionally abandoned and how can the relationship between God's people and the city be reestablished according to God's purposes for both?

Historically, the Church acted as the spine of the city, supporting the community and aiming to steer the people in the right course of direction. Bakke and Roberts write, "These Old First churches were highly sensitive to the social issues prevalent at the time, issues they believed God was leading them to confront . . . Such commitment and zeal for social change had a foundation in the theological orientation of the founders of Old Firsts."[2] The Old First churches of the 19th century remained a constant within changing society. Captivated by the marginalized, they were active in bringing down walls and breaking apart barriers that kept people from working together for the benefit of everyone. These congregations invested in bringing about social change and advocating for positive transformation within their communities. However, as cities continued to expand in areas of trade, commerce and mobility, residency changed from rural upbringings to suburban homes. The dramatic shift

---

1. The use of "Church" throughout the paper may apply to any Christian denomination. However, it most adequately pertains to predominately white Evangelical churches, specifically those who led and contributed to white flight in the last century.

2. Ray Bakke and Sam Roberts, *The Expanded Mission of City Center Churches* (Chicago, IL: International Urban Associates, 1998), 15.

in location would eventually result in "white flight" or the deliberate departure of white, affluent individuals from the city and away from emerging ethnically diverse neighborhoods. Old First congregations were left with the decision to either remain committed to the neighborhoods in which they were located or abandon the very communities that had become their home. Many individuals of the Christian faith willingly chose to participate in the "white-flight" epidemic, moving with the social tide that no longer included the urban neighborhood.

Societal aspirations of individualistic gain and success became the ideal pursuit of the elite and economically advantaged. Jacobsen writes: "people have freely chosen sprawl and all of its trappings with their hard-earned dollars."[3] He explains that the American view of lifestyle includes three core identities: individualism, independence and freedom. Our desire to make decisions on our own, for our own convenience and for our personal benefit, has contributed to the vast disparity between city centers and the surrounding areas. Mobility is a core principle of sprawl that has added to the increasing divide between the marginalized and privileged.

Specifically, cars made possible the opportunity for individuals to move outside city centers and live "comfortably" away from anything that did not fit their way of living. Those in the workforce could live in suburbs and commute into the city. According to Jacobsen, "As cars freed up drivers to live, work, shop and play between farther and farther distances, these great distances became a fixed part of the landscape, making the car necessary for full participation in society."[4] Ability to own a car has become a staple for livelihood, yet many remain excluded from this "necessity." Society continues to foster self-interest over sustainable and interdependent communities.

Urban communities survive in the midst of societal changes that have substantially worked for the benefit and interest of the wealthy and resourced. Oppressive social structures and unequal power dynamics have left the marginalized to cope with the brokenness that is often openly present and working within urban neighborhoods. The Church's absence and neglect fueled economic disparity as well as racial and social divides between the elite white and poor minority groups. The Church's decision to remove itself from the urban neighborhood continues to impact the theological perspective of Christians today, resulting in a distorted understanding of the city.

The Church's general absence in the urban context perpetuated a widening gap between the people of God and the city. Biblical truth concerning the role of the Church within the urban context has been neglected, establishing a selective view of what it means to fully understand and live out the Gospel. Urban missionaries and individuals who have relocated to city centers have purposely chosen to rediscover the city's promise of shalom by becoming intentionally rooted in these communities. It is out of their experiences that many have come to encounter the work of the Holy

3. Eric O. Jacobsen, *Sidewalks in the Kingdom: New Urbanism and the Christian Faith* (Grand Rapids, MI: Brazos, 2003), 29.

4. Ibid, 24.

Spirit within the city, often despite the absence of churches. The connection between God's people and the city remains integral to fully living out the Gospel, affirming the Church's decision to reinvest in the urban neighborhood into which it was called.

Linthicum addresses the source of disconnection between the city and the Church: "It is precisely because the church has failed over the centuries to 'tell the next generation that God is here' that God's people have come to emphasize what is dark and evil about the city and have missed the concrete truth that God is there."[5] Linthicum recognizes that the city has always been a place in which God resides, but people have focused on the brokenness of the city over the good that is there. The Church left the city for self-imposed reasons and has continued to evade the city because of the changes that came about during its time of absence. The Church's inability to see the city as God sees it has resulted in a determined neglect of the city and a detour from the responsibility and investment the Church is to have within the city.

Scripture affirms God's desire for his people to be invested in the city and to ultimately seek the well-being of the land. Jeremiah 29 is a reflection of God's desire for his people to be committed to the places into which he had called them. Specifically, this chapter shows the exile into Babylon as an opportunity for Israel to: "seek the welfare of the city," and in doing so, reap the rewards of their own welfare (Jer. 29:7, ESV). God had called his people to be a presence within a city that he wanted to grow and prosper. While the mandate seemed daunting and unbearable, obedience to the command would mean that Babylon and Israel would both flourish. Bakke writes: "God is not asking the exiles to lead a passive, patient existence in the enemy city. He's asking that they actively work for Babylon's shalom, that is, peace with justice. Moreover, the promise is that they and presumably their families will be blessed thereby."[6] God called Israel to seek the well-being of Babylon and there is still a command for God's people to actively participate in God's work in the city for the overall transformation of both individuals and communities.

Genuine transformation of the cities of America requires the pursuit of God's shalom. Bakke explains: "you are never more like God than when you are living in relationship with God's people and working in partnerships for the re-creation and redemption of God's world."[7] According to Bakke, the Church is to be in partnership with the community to help bring about God's work in the city. Shalom happens in the gathering of worship, work and fellowship with one another. The reality that everything is as it should be is manifested in the coming together of a community for the well-being of the city and its people. Bakke and Roberts write: "Mission involves everything the church does in response to God's creative and redemptive mandates . . . Discipleship, stewardship, and fellowship, like evangelism and social

---

5. Robert C. Linthicum, *City of God, City of Satan: A Biblical Theology of the Urban Church* (Grand Rapids, MI: Zondervan, 1991), 33.

6. Ray Bakke, *A Theology as Big as the City* (Downers Grove, IL: InterVarsity, 1997), 85.

7. Bakke, *A Theology*, 35.

responsibility, deal with specific and concrete actions."[8] Therefore, shalom becomes a by-product of intentional mission.

However, to reach a place where mission is possible within the city, the Church must work towards reconciliation between itself and the city. Obstacles and challenges that arose out of abandonment must be addressed by the Church. Reintegration into the urban neighborhood will require recognition of past faults and mistakes in order to foster growth and trust. The city has learned to operate and function as its own entity largely without the support of the Church. Entry back into the city will demand characteristics of consistency and intentionality. Respect will need to be earned and honor to be given for the good within the city.

Another perspective the Church should maintain is that of God's sovereignty. The Church is not going into the city to "save" the city. Rather, the Church has the opportunity to partner with God in the work that God is already doing within the community. God's presence in the city is more than enough to keep the city moving forward into relationship with God. Still, God desires to use the Church in God's ministry of reconciliation. The decision to reinvest in the city will require unity among those in the city and those coming back into the neighborhood. This opportune season of growth and transformation can result in a renewed ability to reinvest in the cities and inner cities of America, while also learning from the urban community.

The ways in which the Church is able to reestablish its presence in the city will look different than the Church's early beginnings. The "white flight" decision acted as a great disservice to the city and Church. Not only did churches abandon the places into which God had called them, but they ultimately contributed to the disconnection that occurred across ethnic, social and economic lines within our own borders. These challenges and conflicts should act as motivation to pursue right relationship with God and people. Genuine relationship with the people of the city is one of the greatest ways to be present in the urban neighborhood. To build trust with people means to eventually earn trust with the communities to which they belong.

In the initial steps of reintegrating into the urban neighborhood, support and encouragement are characteristics that should be highly pursued. The Church should find ways in which it can come alongside organizations, invested individuals, and other congregations who are already present within the city. The Church should be willing to learn about the community in which they are choosing to invest and how particular groups have already begun to shape, lead and resource the community. Rather than coming in with an agenda about the ways in which a particular church can contribute its resources and sense of identity, a period of being consistently present within the community will reveal a genuine desire to know the city and build relationship with the people. The Church can then work toward incarnational mission in the city.

---

8. Bakke and Roberts, *The Expanded Mission*, 85.

According to Jacobsen, presence is merely the beginning step to becoming intentionally rooted in city centers. He writes: "our cities require not only presence, but targeted mission efforts."[9] Intentional efforts may include relocation for those who feel called to live in urban communities, the empowerment of community members through informational meetings and educational resources, or invested advocacy on behalf of those who are unable to speak for themselves. God's command to seek the well-being of the community (Jer. 29:7) is essential to uncovering the ways in which the Church is still relevant to the city. It is out of genuine trust and relationship, intentional investment and biblical understanding, and reverence for Scripture that true reconciliation can become a reality and genuine community can flourish.

BIBLIOGRAPHY

Bakke, Ray. *A Theology as Big as the City.* Downers Grove, IL: InterVarsity Press, 1997.

Bakke, Ray and Sam Roberts. *The Expanded Mission of City Center Churches.* Chicago, IL: International Urban Associates, 1998.

Jacobsen, Eric O. *Sidewalks in the Kingdom: New Urbanism and the Christian Faith.* Grand Rapids, MI: Brazos Press, 2003.

Linthicum, Robert C. *City of God, City of Satan: A Biblical Theology of the Urban Church.* Grand Rapids, MI: Zondervan, 1991.

9. Jacobsen, *Sidewalks in the Kingdom*, 16.

Part II

CCDA Ministry in North Carolina

NORTH CAROLINA'S CRY FOR RACIAL JUSTICE

REYNOLDS CHAPMAN

Jeremiah 29:7 is a fitting theme verse for the CCDA conference. The concept of *shalom,* the word that is translated as "peace" or "welfare" in the passage, captures CCDA's foundational three R's—relocation, reconciliation, and redistribution. What makes CCDA unique is its emphasis that all R's are essential. This is rooted in God's emphasis that peace is not peace without justice, and that peace and justice come about through God's presence and the presence of the people of God. The conference theme, "Flourish", is a hearkening to God's robust vision for comprehensive wholeness in the cities where we find ourselves in exile.

North Carolina's blind spot is a product of compartmentalizing the three R's. I have seen this mostly from the context of my own city of Durham. It is a place where there has historically been a relative absence of public conflict, but where the inequalities are deeply ingrained in the life of the city. There has been peace without justice. Since its early years, Durham has been heralded as a place of good relations between people of different races. Or as a journalist put it in 1925, Durham was "distinguished by mutual politeness," and by "little public friction between the races."[1] Now our Convention and Visitor's Bureau calls us "a diverse, open, and tolerant community, with power shared among various ethnic groups."[2]

Durham has seen an economic boom in recent years, along with many other parts of North Carolina. In the Triangle region (Raleigh, Durham, and Chapel Hill) there are twelve universities—including three tier-1 research universities—and Research Triangle Park, a hub of innovation and industry. Together, rapid economic

---

1. Osha Gray Davidson, *The Best of Enemies* (Chapel Hill, NC: The University of North Carolina Press, 1996), 28.

2. "25 Water-Cooler Fables About Durham and the Realities Behind Them," *Durham Convention & Visitors Bureau*, Internet, available from http://www.durham-nc.com/resources/pdf/25Water-Cooler_Fables.pdf.

growth and a progressive self-concept make the Triangle, and much of North Carolina, a beacon of the New South.

But this veneer of progress has allowed us to ignore and hide the suffering and ill-treatment of those who do not have access to the opportunities NC has to offer. Jeremiah responded to a similar atmosphere in Israel by saying "They have treated the wound of my people carelessly, saying 'peace, peace, when there is no peace'" (6:14). And what was the people's response? They tried to kill him. They wanted their prophets to say nice things so they could feel good about themselves and continue being "greedy for unjust gain" (6:13). When God's people are complacent with a truncated view of God's vision of *shalom* for our cities, we need a prophet like Jeremiah to turn the lights on.

God's robust vision of *shalom* informs our response to the racialized realities in Durham and in our state of North Carolina. Claims of racial bias have been a big part of public political discussion in the last couple years. In response to calls for justice, our leaders have hidden themselves behind hollow understandings of race. There are two movements happening right now in NC that are seeking a vision of "flourishing" for *all* of our neighbors in a society that has been conditioned to allow only some to flourish.

North Carolina is fortunate to have extensive documentation of law enforcement patterns. This has helped a professor at UNC show that drug enforcement in Durham, NC, significantly reflects racial bias. Although marijuana usage rates are the roughly the same amongst blacks and whites in Durham, black motorists in our city are twice more likely to be searched from traffic stops than whites. Blacks are four times more likely to be arrested for marijuana possession than whites. In response to unequal law enforcement in Durham, we have started a grassroots coalition of attorneys, community leaders, and church leaders called Fostering Alternative Drug Enforcement (FADE).

As we have learned from people like Michelle Alexander, who spoke at last year's CCDA conference, the long-term impact of a drug conviction is devastating. I have seen persistent, hard-working people in my neighborhood continually held back from a job because of their criminal record. I have also seen the police hold up my neighbor for an hour right outside my door, calling for backup and searching him with dogs because he did not come to a complete stop at a stop sign. Just down the street at Duke University drugs are rampant in their party culture, but the police are not making arrests there.

FADE formed to turn the lights on—to publicize the unequal enforcement of drug laws and hold the Durham Police Department (DPD) accountable. We have been clear to say that there is racial bias in the DPD, and we gave them a list of suggestions for how to make law enforcement more racially just.

But the response from the DPD has shown how harmful an inadequate view of peace can be. They have denied that there is racial bias in their law enforcement, and pointed to the diversity in the police department as evidence. They are equating racial diversity with racial justice. They see people with different colored skin living and working together and assume that such a picture is what makes life good for everyone. This posture is what makes Durham "America's most tolerant city" (according to the Daily Beast), while at the same time making black neighborhoods afraid of, rather than protected by, police. We may not tolerate hate crimes, but we tolerate our whole justice system being infected with racism. We are so tolerant that we allow our leaders to oppress our minority neighborhoods.

Like the false prophets in Jeremiah's day, the leaders in our city are saying "'peace, peace,' when there is no peace." The FADE coalition is saying that real peace is more than having a diverse police department. We are advocating for a vision of *shalom* where not only do people of different races live and work together, but also where they have the same opportunities and treatment.

In North Carolina, the Forward Together movement has been another arena for challenging the harmful effects of racial bias. The weekly "Moral Monday" protests led by Rev. Dr. William Barber and the NC NAACP have revealed that the NC legislature was seeking to pass laws that silenced and encumbered minorities. The legislators repealed the Racial Justice Act, which sought to minimize the sentencing if race played a factor in a conviction. They instituted a rigid voting law that cut opportunities to vote in areas where minorities were proportionately high—early voting, same-day registration, out-of-precinct ballots, with non-state-issued ID. And they pulled public education funding to put it into a voucher system that would help parents pay to send their kids to private school—the vast majority of whom are white. These were just a few of the more obvious laws that instituted severe subjugation of minorities.

What has been happening in the NC legislature has shown how privilege can both create and sustain a legal structure that makes minorities second-class citizens. When privileged people in power make decisions for people and communities they neither know nor live with, they have a hard time seeing how people who do not share their privileges are affected. NC Senator Tom Apodaca called the voting rights act—a result of the civil rights struggle to prevent discrimination in voting—a "headache." He and his colleagues who supported its repeal do not seem to recognize how much of a headache it is to be denied participation in a so-called "democracy" on the basis of your skin color. It is easy to miss this in a political and social silo away from communities that bear the burden of harmful legislation. But CCDA's *shalom* vision of the three R's emphasizes that God's presence among people who are disenfranchised is foundational for "seeking the peace of the city." Supporting policies based on principles that are abstracted from directly affected communities comes from isolation and a thin understanding of the common good.

But the Forward Together movement also helped me realize that living in a low-wealth community does not cleanse me of my privilege. I know this because I almost missed the movement. I was busy doing the "work of the Lord" as a local minister, setting up small groups and planning mission initiatives intended to "seek the peace of the city." I had no idea what was going on in the NC legislature. Why? Because the laws that were being written and signed did not directly affect me. In fact, it took me a couple months before I even attended the Moral Mondays rallies.

I was part of North Carolina's blind spot—feeling good about altruistic causes but unaware of the principalities and powers that create the need for benevolence. Situations like this make people like me double-heroes on the backs of poor and subjugated communities—we use our privilege to become successful (whether it be business, ministry—whatever), and then use our position of power to help a few poor people emerge from poverty. I was operating out of an incomplete vision of *shalom*—one that was living out relocation and reconciliation without a full vision for redistribution. I failed to recognize that basic opportunities for education, health care, and voting were being unequally distributed.

After a summer of being "too busy" to think about participating in the Moral Mondays' civil disobedience, my brother-in-law asked if I wanted to participate with him at the last one. I realized that I needed to pray about it, and I took a day to sit on it. Once I did, I realized that there was no way to spin the legislature's actions as being beneficial to minorities. It was an outright affront. Civil disobedience was a way to turn the lights on and put pressure on leaders to do something different. So I decided to get arrested in the legislative building as a statement that the laws being passed were not just.

The privilege of the lawmakers was a partner with my privilege as a citizen. They had the power to create the laws, and I had the power to ignore them. As these two forces worked together, those without power lost their education funding, a fair trial, and the opportunity to vote. North Carolina needs a vision of *shalom*. We need a grasp of the permeating effects of sin—the understanding that sin is in our hearts, our land, and our government. And we also need to see that God's calling—and ultimately God's redemption in Jesus Christ—heals all of the sin that causes people to suffer. Only when everyone is flourishing can we say there is peace in our city.

BIBLIOGRAPHY

"25 Water-Cooler Fables About Durham and the Realities Behind Them." *Durham Convention & Visitors Bureau*. Internet. Available from http://www.durham-nc.com/resources/pdf/25Water-Cooler_Fables.pdf.

Davidson, Osha Gray. *The Best of Enemies*. Chapel Hill, NC: The University of North Carolina Press, 1996.

LITURGICAL GARDENING

ANATHOTH COMMUNITY GARDEN AND FARM AS A PLACE OF WORSHIP AND COMMUNITY DEVELOPMENT

CHAS EDENS

There is a growing awareness that the flourishing of human and non-human creation is inextricably linked, and that eating and growing good food together is a faithful way to foster reconciliation between neighbors and the land. One manifestation of this trend is the various community garden projects that continue to crop up in neighborhoods and on church lots. As the director of one of these projects—Anathoth Community Garden and Farm in Cedar Grove, NC—I have been trying to discern how our work fits within the larger framework of CCDA, particularly within a rural context. In doing so, I have found it helpful to see our community garden: (1) as a place of worship, and (2) as an approach to rural community development.

The impetus for Anathoth originated in 2004 when a man named Bill King was shot and killed at his corner grocery store. The impetus was even more urgent eight years later when Phillip Johnson and Skip Wade were also murdered at the same store in an apparent robbery. For a quiet, seemingly quaint, town, three murders in the span of eight years presented a shocking reminder that the divisions in this rural community, and many other rural communities, are usually just obscured to those who live outside of a rural context. The interdependent family farms that once quilted the landscape have mostly been replaced by the markings of industrial agriculture, wealth accrued from the surrounding cities, or poverty. Chicken houses stretch the length of football fields, and are accompanied by tattered trailers that provide shelter for the migrant laborers who work in them. A relatively new housing development surrounds the county reservoir and protrudes with suburban-style houses and immaculately-kept lawns like an oasis in the desert. In between these there are many other people living down gravel drives or next to high-speed roadways, coping with disability, disease, joblessness, old age through the excessive consumption of television, drugs, or lottery tickets.

When a crime occurs in a rural community a self-assigned community-watch volunteer with a police scanner covers the news if the local media does not cover it. The perpetrators are recognizable. Gas stations sell printouts of monthly mug shots from the local police station. This is supposedly as an effort to reduce recidivism in the justice system, but more likely (and more lucratively) because differentiating Them from Us plays into the larger and more elusive aims of the principalities and powers. These crimes and categorized criminals serve to justify the political skepticism and religious conviction that many rural people subscribe to, and increasingly, cling to. The growing consensus is that entitlement checks and philanthropic handouts have spawned a culture of lazy sinners who are intent on stealing tax dollars and house-wares from hard-working Christians. This is the narrative of scarcity and fear that sells home security systems and elects politicians; it deepens the divisions between neighbors and their place.

But after Bill King's murder in 2004 more than 100 residents of Cedar Grove decided to respond in a different manner. Farm owners and farmworkers, rich and poor, saved and unsaved, us and them, attended a peace vigil that was organized by an African-American man named Valee Taylor and a white woman named Grace Hackney. Valee's family descended from sharecroppers and had inherited land adjacent to the store. Grace was the pastor of Cedar Grove United Methodist Church, located two miles down the road. At the vigil, Valee's mother Scenobia received a divine vision to donate a parcel of her family's land to the community, and Pastor Grace suggested that the gifted land could take the shape of a community garden. With Scenobia's blessing, the land was deeded to the church and garden beds were dug in the fall of that year by a group of volunteers. Named Anathoth, our ministry derives its name from the biblical story in which Jeremiah purchases a field (at Anathoth) and tells the Israelites to "plant gardens" and "seek peace" (Jer. 29: 7, 9). The correlation between Jeremiah's gift and Scenobia's gift was a prophetic act that overturned the existing (dis)order of power and continues to summon us to embody a life together that is sustained by peace.

It is in the sense that the work of gardening at Anathoth is a "process of formation that aims our desires, primes our imagination, and orients us to the world,"[1] that it can be understood primarily as a place of worship. One might even say that Anathoth is a *correction* of Christian worship in a Bible-belt culture where it has too often gone awry. Health-and-wealth morality, pie-in-the-sky spirituality, and get-right-with-God triumphalism are so common in entertainment and therapy driven church worship. These downgrade the significance of Jesus' incarnation and his ministry to bodies, and thus orient people away from the material concerns of the surrounding neighborhood. Anathoth, however, represents a mode of worship that is bound with the material world. As Wendell Berry puts it, "When we [garden] knowingly, lovingly, skillfully,

---

1. James K.A. Smith, *Desiring the Kingdom: Worship, Worldview and Cultural Formation* (Grand Rapids, MI: Baker Academic, 2009), 39–40.

reverently, it is a sacrament."[2] Therefore, like any good Christian liturgy, tending the garden engrains into the vision and muscle memory a reverence before God and a delight for the world in all of its particularity. The exercise of making compost not only facilitates the decomposition of crop residue and straw into humus but it also instills a posture of *humility*, or rather, the offering of one's body as a living sacrifice. Weeding a bed of broccoli, waiting for the season's first tomato to ripen, or sharing a potluck meal, reorients people away from the lie of competition and narcissism. Rather, these exercises orient people toward the promise that flourishing is possible on earth as it is in heaven, inside of creaturely limitation and responsibility.

Outside of understanding Anathoth in liturgical terms, our ministry also represents a profound practical way to reconcile with problems that are embedded in this community's complicated history. The legacy of racial and class tension, and ecological degradation is more palpable in a rural community where white and African American neighbors sometimes share the same surname that originated in a slave economy, and where acres of tobacco continue to rape the soil of its fertility.[3] At its best, Anathoth confronts this ruptured history by standing inside of it and modeling an alternative economic exchange that extends from our posture of worship. Our ministry now includes a satellite farm a few miles down the road and centers on a sliding-scale Community Supported Agriculture (CSA) program called HarvestShare. HarvestShare's goal is to involve the community in the work of gardening while making good food accessible to folks with varying income levels in and around Cedar Grove. Participants pay at the beginnings of the season at a level that they can afford; some are churches or church-folk who donate a share, some are students or single parents who purchase a share for themselves and others are widows confined to their home who receive a hand-delivered box at no cost. The weekly boxes are sized according to the number of people in a household and are comprised of a bounty of seasonal

2. Wendell Berry and Norman Wirzba, *The Art of the Commonplace: Agrarian Essays of Wendell Berry* (Washington, D.C.: Counterpoint, 2002), 304.

3. Perhaps the primary reason that religious and political extremism is often born and bred in rural communities, domestically and abroad, is not because rural people are simple-minded and unable to, for example, grasp the concept of a liberal democracy or contextualize scripture. Rather, it is because of the immediacy of their relationships with each other and the land that has historically been mediated by agriculture. It may be harder for rural people to imagine a rationale or political order that is overly abstract or nuanced when the character of every other relationship is more direct, personal and literal. The agro-economic framework in which rural people are embedded necessitates the directness of speech and understanding. While this does not dismiss or excuse scriptural interpretations that can sometimes manifest as xenophobia and violence, it does suggest an alternative way to read rural people that is more charitable and even indebted. More specifically, the groundswell of Jesus' ministry is, in part, attributed to the fact that it gained momentum in rural communities. The interesting point here is that wherever rural communities are portrayed as the setting of backwards fundamentalism, they also represent the place of Jesus' ministry where so many of his miracles and his parables about seeds and soil were contextualized in ways that would resonate with rural people. Therefore, Christian leaders would do well to learn from rural people how to relate to the world in such a way that the Gospel can be radicalized.

fruits, vegetables, and often wood oven-baked bread. Participants are encouraged to join us for community workdays that are held twice a week and also to share a potluck meal together afterwards.

With the assistance of grant funding and additional donations, the cost of each share corresponds with the amount of seeds, packaging, fuel, and soil amendments required to grow and distribute the weekly boxes. The funding from HarvestShare also enables us to support high-school age and adult interns with the opportunity to learn how to grow food using organic methods and incorporate food and agriculture into their ministry. The local teenagers we employ are paid an hourly wage, and they work part-time during the school year and more regularly during the summer. Our adult interns come from Duke Divinity School and many other colleges and seminaries around the country for ten weeks during the summer. Many of the adults live in (domestic) community with a host family in Cedar Grove, and throughout the summer they follow a curriculum that facilitates a reflection on different theological and practical aspects of our ministry. This summer, for instance, a weekly section of theological readings and reflection might be entitled, "Reckoning with the Inherent Privilege of Downward Mobility," accompanied by a practical section entitled, "Seed Propagation 101." Our goal for the adult internship is to equip emerging leaders (or as I like to say, emerging *weeders*) with the imagination and skillset to better minister to all of the creatures in their own neighborhood.

Finally, it is easy to romanticize Anathoth as a slice of paradise where people from all walks of life come to work in harmony with nature. Even I have this temptation in my appeal to volunteers, interns, and donors (even to myself). But the reality is often short of the vision. The summers are sticky and hot, the walk-in cooler is currently undersized and malfunctioning, communication lines between staff, interns, and volunteers get tired and strained, and worst of all some neighbors feel legitimately excluded for one reason or another. The most extreme feedback we have gotten has sounded something like: "How dare these self-righteous city slickers preach to us about organic gardening!" I regularly hear of even neighbors who are not aware of Anathoth's existence. These less glamorous realities deserve at least as many words of reflection and repentance. As such, our days begin with prayers of praise and concern, and a space for mutual admonition and confession amongst the group. Sometimes my favorite prayers are those in which we sit still and listen to our breath and the stirring of the garden around us. At those times, I silently ask that we may receive each other and every part of creation as we truly are: gifts from God.

BIBLIOGRAPHY

Berry, Wendell and Norman Wirzba. *The Art of the Commonplace: Agrarian Essays of Wendell Berry*. Washington, D.C.: Counterpoint, 2002.

Smith, James K.A. *Desiring the Kingdom: Worship, Worldview and Cultural Formation*. Grand Rapids, MI: Baker Academic, 2009.

Part III

Book Reviews

Forgive Us: Confessions of a Compromised Faith by Mae Elise Cannon, Lisa
Sharon Harper, Troy Jackson and Soong-Chan Rah.
Grand Rapids, MI: Zondervan, 2004. 240 pages.
Reviewed by Margot Starbuck

I *started* reading "Forgive Us" because I knew I should.

Sort of like eating dark-green leafy vegetables.

Like many American Christians, I'm vaguely aware that Evangelical Christianity
in America has sinned in our treatment of minorities, women, homosexuals, followers of other religions and others who don't fit the tight religious molds we've created.

And like many, I feel bad about that.

By "bad," of course, I mean the kind of "bad" I feel after eating half a dozen
Krispy Kreme donuts. Repeatedly. I feel bad for a moment, but I don't really change
my behavior.

Before I cracked the binding, I knew that the authors of *Forgive Us* wouldn't let
me off the hook because I felt bad. There would be, I expected, a recipe for change.

In addition to my marginal sense of moral obligation, I also read *Forgive Us* because, as a privileged person within Evangelical culture, I knew that these particular
writers could help me understand what I did not yet see. If I had to be reeducated—
which, of course, I did—there was no one I'd rather be schooled by than Cannon,
Harper, Jackson and Rah. I already valued their wisdom and trusted that they would
speak the truth in love. They'd butter the greens.

And to be honest, that *Forgive Us* had been published by Zondervan Academic
did make me a little bit itchy to see how the authors would walk the thin wire: both
critiquing and guiding the Evangelical church. Because I expected rigorous truth-tell-
ing from these four, I was curious how they'd serve it up so that a largely Evangelical
audience could stomach the truth.

The burdensome sense of moral responsibility, the dream team of authors and a
bit of curiosity got me to open the book.

Once I got a taste, I wanted more.

The authors—that I actually like to think of as the theological version of Marvel's
popular Avengers superheroes—drew me in with excellent writing. In each chapter, a
unique story of privilege and power, with compelling historical detail, unfolds. These

narratives give reliable substance to some of the vague fuzzy notions American Evangelical Christians like me—certain that *someone else* is to blame—have about *why* we've become known as those who exclude the ones that God loves.

And while I'd naively expected each author to mount, one after the next, chapter by chapter, the cliche soapbox I'd so thoughtlessly assigned to each—"woman," "black," "Asian," etc.—I was delighted to discover that the authors have written with a unified voice throughout. This cross-pollination, raising our voices to advocate *together* for those who are "other" than we are, of course, *models* the very message these authors are so effectively communicating. Together they model the reality that the pain which the church has caused isn't ever "their pain;" it is "*our* pain."

Within the first few pages, I couldn't put this book down.

The authors write, "Many Christians today are unaware of the events that mark the American church's greatest tragedies." Unaware, I simply didn't know to include myself in this group *until* I'd read this book. Chapter by chapter I began to understand more fully how the church has been complicit in both ravaging the environment and in marginalizing those within and outside of the church who are beloved by God.

Graciously, the authors do not leave readers like me *stuck feeling bad*. Rather, they provide a path to real release through the power of confession, the necessary first step to systemic change.

Don't read this book because it's good for you. Read it because it's delicious. *Forgive Us* is a compelling, well-written volume that is certain to be instrumental in the church finally becoming who we were made to be.

Too Heavy a Yoke: Black Women and the Burden of Strength by Chanequa Walker-Barnes. Eugene, OR: Cascade, 2014. 209 pages. Reviewed by Nilwona E. Nowlin

Being a black woman who is strong can be commendable, but being a StrongBlack-Woman can be dangerous. Chanequa Walker-Barnes describes the StrongBlackWoman as a black woman who consistently puts others before herself, even at the expense of her own physical and psychological well-being (4). The StrongBlackWoman lives out her existence in the world through the display of emotional strength/regulation, caregiving, and independence. These traits are not specific to StrongBlackWomen, black women or women, for that matter; nor are they inherently bad traits. The problem arises when they exist in excess instead of moderation, as is the case for the StrongBlackWoman (18). Walker-Barnes holds multiple degrees and is trained in the areas of psychology, clinical psychology, African American studies, theology, ministry and gender. In addition, she currently serves as the Associate Professor of Pastoral Care and Counseling at McAfee School of Theology (Mercer University) and has experience as a licensed clinical psychologist and pastoral counselor. Years of professional research contribute to this book, but her expertise also comes from her own experience as a self-proclaimed recovering StrongBlackWoman. In addition to her personal experience and research, Walker-Barnes presents the lived experiences of other black women as authoritative sources. This combination of sources contributes to a fuller and more authentic discussion.

In her introduction, Walker-Barnes states that the StrongBlackWoman is not the problem but a symptom of a larger problem. It is one of a handful of stereotypical archetypes created by society over generations. The terms *StrongBlackWoman* and "strong black woman" began to appear in literature about twelve years ago, and most writers have presented it as black women's attempt to cope with the pressures of life while finding themselves at a higher risk for physical and psychological distress. She critiques these writers' works because they are not in conversation with each other, and their conversations have not often dealt explicitly with pastoral theology and practice. Walker-Barnes believes that the Christian church has participated in constructing and reinforcing this ideology, so it has a responsibility to dismantle the walls that have imprisoned generations of black women. Her book sets out to equip those who are willing to accept the responsibility and the challenge by increasing "pastoral awareness and discourse about the inordinate burden that the demand for *strength* places upon women of African descent" (8). Specifically, it is intended for pastoral theologians, pastoral caregivers and Christian mental health workers who provide services to black women.

Walker-Barnes presents her case using a fourfold mission:

1. Describe the beliefs, thoughts, and behaviors that are characteristic of the Strong-BlackWoman and the impact of this myth upon the physical, emotional, and relational health of the women who emulate it.

2. Explain the functions of this myth in American society, providing the reader with a new understanding of how the archetype originated and how it continues to be reinforced.

3. Highlight the unique significance of this phenomenon for the Christian church and the responsibility of pastoral caregivers in confronting and alleviating its existence.

4. Provide a model for liberative pastoral care with StrongBlackWomen (8).

In addition, Walker-Barnes uses a womanist methodology and intersectional analyses in order to understand how race, gender, and religion impact the black woman's reality in the present day. This awareness is a crucial part of any attempt to provide effective pastoral care for a StrongBlackWoman.

Whether or not they are conscious of it, most black women are socialized from birth to live into the identity of a strong, black woman. They are applauded for their ability to endure varying degrees of physical and emotional pain, to bear the weight of the world on their shoulders. However, Walker-Barnes points out that the coping mechanisms that are usually employed eventually prove to be detrimental to a black woman's overall well-being. It turns out that these generations of black women are not living into the positive identity of a strong, black woman at all. Instead, they have fallen into the trap of its dangerous "evil twin sister," the StrongBlackWoman. Walker-Barnes spends a significant amount of time tracing the genealogy of the archetype of the StrongBlackWoman, which is born out of black women's attempt to "defend against the negative representations of their identities by White racism" (11). It was the counternarrative to images such as the Mammy, the Jezebel and the matriarch. She also discusses the relationship between the archetype of the StrongBlackWoman and the cult of true womanhood—the white, middle class ideal that held up piety, purity, domesticity and submissiveness as the traits of a "true" woman, traits that could only be possessed by white women.

Walker-Barnes also explains how the Christian church—the black church in particular—has contributed to the problem more than it has provided a solution. The church often holds up the StrongBlackWoman as the standard and fails to acknowledge that most black women are killing themselves softly. She frames her discussion of the theological and pastoral implications through the lens of the Greatest Commandment. In addition to loving God, we are commanded to love our neighbor *as ourselves*. In reinforcing this archetype, the church is complicit in the violation of this commandment (12). She concludes the book by framing the ideology of the Strong-BlackWoman as an addiction and proposes a pastoral intervention with a twelve-step recovery process as its foundation. She also provides a clear model based on this process.

One challenge of this book is that, though it is written for the pastoral practitioner, its academic language could become a barrier to some. One practical highlight of the book that might help balance this out is the "suggestions for pastoral practice" provided at the end of each chapter. This encourages the reader to take the time to consider how they can apply the book to their particular context. While the book is most accessible to those with prior knowledge of how gender, race and religion can negatively impact black women, Walker-Barnes does a thorough job of presenting the facts to those who may not be as well-versed in this area.

As a black woman, this reviewer had to pause, re-read and sometimes put down the book multiple times because the facts and narratives hit so close to home. Walker-Barnes tells some hard but necessary truths and provides a practical, possible path toward healing and wholeness.

Faith Rooted Organizing: Mobilizing the Church in Service to the World by Alexia Salvatierra and Peter Heltzel. Downers Grove, IL: InterVarsity Press, 2014. 2018 pages. Reviewed by Anthony Grimes.

Authors Alexia Salvatierra and Peter Heltzel have situated *Faith-Rooted Organizing: Mobilizing the Church in Service to the World* in the center of two opposite hesitancies: an evangelicalism that has, at times, been hesitant to engage social issues in their most complicated socio-political manifestations and secular organizing models that have been hesitant to embrace the moral force of faith-led movements. The result is a potent resource that provides not only the motivation, but also the philosophical framework for a community organizing "way of life" that is saturated in the Christian faith tradition (12).

Whether aware consciously or not, most community organizing models are based on the methodology of Saul Alinsky, the Chicago based organizer of the 1930s, whose legacy is one of mobilizing the underprivileged against power structures through very intense, sternly focused, and often unsustainable coalitions. Alinksy's principles have been adapted by faith communities who employ "faith-based" strategies of organizing and advocacy. However, few have tried, as these authors have, to develop a completely *faith-rooted* approach to organizing which draws upon diverse Christian traditions that shape and guide the entire process. In doing so, Salvatierra and Heltzel draw upon their pastoral and organizing experience to reshape six core areas of classic organizing: goals, analysis, strategies, recruitment, leadership development, and sustainability.

The book masterfully answers the following questions: what do faith traditions uniquely add to community organizing? Why are the faith traditions essential for advocacy work? What is the biblical basis for organizing and advocacy? Most notably, the authors demonstrate how "faith-rooted" organizing is about discerning which issues to engage (rather than choosing them according to self-interests), following the lead of a God who flips power dynamics in the kingdom, and seeking to be connected to faith communities who use disciplines that personally sustain and equip organizers.

The authors impressively use a wide array of stories from the freedom movements of North America and, even more uniquely, from movements based in the global south and among indigenous people-groups to illustrate their points. *Faith-Rooted Organizing* benefits, then, from utilizing such a rich global perspective. There is a refreshing character to a book which continually emphasizes the importance of "seeing from below" and actually includes the perspectives of our global partners who indeed live from below. The reader is provided with useful historical snapshots and metaphors that inform him or her in invigorating ways.

The book is perhaps lacking, mostly due to several lacunae that, at times, leave it lost between different genres of literature. The book lacks a devotional character that would make it, as the authors propose in the beginning, a true orientating guide for forming a Christian "way of life" around organizing. It also lacks some of the practicality of a "how to guide" and the biblical depth of a theological standard. Because of these missing parts, perhaps omitted due to space limitations, the book cannot possibly stand on its own without supplemental organizing resources. One could view these critiques as a plea for Salvatierra and Heltzel to say even more!

Overall, I highly recommend this resource for veteran organizers who need to be reminded of the special role their faith plays in community organizing as well as for those who are new to the complex landscape of advocacy. *Faith-Rooted Organizing* could potentially serve as a framework for the Spirit's work in leading the evangelical church beyond charity to concrete systemic change.

www.ingramcontent.com/pod-product-compliance
Lightning Source LLC
Chambersburg PA
CBHW081141090426
42736CB00018B/3437